The F Word

How we learned to swear by feminism

Jane Caro & Catherine Fox

NEW
SOUTH

A New South book

Published by
University of New South Wales Press Ltd
University of New South Wales
Sydney NSW 2052
AUSTRALIA
www.unswpress.com.au

© Jane Caro and Catherine Fox 2008
First published 2008

National Library of Australia
Cataloguing-in-Publication entry

   Title: The F word: how we learned to swear by feminism /authors,
           Jane Caro; Catherine Fox.
   Publisher: Sydney: University of N.S.W., 2008.
   ISBN: 978 086840 823 1 (pbk.)
   Notes: Includes index.
   Subjects: Feminism.
                  Quality of work life.
                  Sex discrimination against women.
                  Work and family.
                  Male domination (Social structure).
   Dewey Number: 305.42

Design Josephine Pajor-Markus
Cover Boheem Design
Author photograph Hilary Cam
Printer Ligare

This book is printed on paper using fibre supplied from plantation or sustainably managed
forests.

The F Word

Jane Caro is an award-winning advertising writer, a frequent media commentator on advertising, marketing, parenting and education for Channel 7 *Sunrise,* and appears on a semi-regular basis in Richard Glover's political forum on 702 ABC Sydney. She has written for mainstream newspapers and is a regular columnist for *New Matilda* and *Education Review*. She is the co-author with Chris Bonnor of *The Stupid Country: How Australia is dismantling public education* (New South, 2007). She is a part-time lecturer (Advertising Creative) in The School of Communication Arts at UWS, a beef producer, a timber grower, a wife and the mother of two teenagers.

Catherine Fox is deputy editor of *AFR Boss* magazine and writes a weekly column, 'Corporate Woman', for the *Australian Financial Review*. She has worked in financial marketing and consulting in Sydney and London and is a regular speaker at seminars and conferences around the country. She is co-author with Helen Trinca of *Better than Sex: How a whole generation got hooked on work* (2004), which was shortlisted for the Blake Dawson Waldron Business Book of the Year award. Her journalism has won several awards. Catherine lives in Sydney with her husband and three daughters.

To our parents:
Kate & Andy, Patricia & John

Contents

Introduction

Virginia Woolf famously claimed that women needed a 'room of their own' before they could fulfil their talent and potential. And indeed such a luxury would be nice. But even today, in our ever-expanding houses, how many women have a room entirely to themselves? If there is a study, it is a communal one. Even in the workplace, offices have gone open-plan. Of course, Woolf's point was as much about mental space as it was about an actual room, and technology has given us something she would surely have envied. Computers have given busy women, particularly mothers, the ability to create a virtual room of their own, and to access instantly the world's great libraries. Without these, the discipline and logistics required to write this book – or any other, for that matter – would probably have been beyond us. We owe a debt of gratitude therefore to the inventors of the microchip.

As we wrote this book, we have each continued to run houses, look after kids, cook, clean and hold down a job or run a business. We wrote this, separately and together, at kitchen tables, on our knees, commuting to work and at each other's houses. We've done it surrounded by children, pets, phone calls, emails and tradesmen, serenaded by pounding rock music and blaring TV. When Mum is writing a book she remains on call. That's reality and it has its benefits. After all, we're writing about our lives and living them at the same time. It's much harder for women — particularly if they have children — to draw strict boundaries around their work, so we have simply learnt to do without them (the boundaries, that is, not the childbirth). Sure, to get our attention as we struggled with a particularly knotty problem our kids have had to call us quite a few times — at ever-increasing volume. Just to add to the confusion, of course, both of us answer to 'Mum'.

The irony of writing a book amid the bustle of domesticity hasn't escaped us. This is a book about feminism, after all. But it's not a theoretical book; it's about us — our friends, our lives and our conversations. It's about how feminism has affected our lives and how, in defiance of its critics, continues to improve, enhance and enrich us. Feminism hasn't solved every problem but that's no reason to pronounce it a failure. When we look at the messy, demanding, rich, difficult and exciting lives that women like us are able to lead today, we wouldn't trade them for the limitations of women's roles in previous generations.

It is, however, scary to be responsible for yourself and to make your own choices. As Simone de Beauvoir warned us, liberty brings anxiety and feminism is about change and freedom. When that angst is combined with a society-wide fear of an unpredictable future it's less surprising feminism has become the F word. Nevertheless, as feminists, we believe that women are of equal value to men and entitled to the same rights and the same range of choices and opportunities, and we don't believe anything about that core definition has changed. We swear by feminism, not at it.

Some who read this book will call us old-fashioned, and dismiss us as classic over-privileged baby boomers. Some will go further and accuse us of being anti-men. It always surprises us that every time we express a pro-feminist (or even pro-female) opinion, we run the risk of being labelled man-haters. Nothing could be further from the truth. There are as many men in the world as there are women that we love, admire and delight in. When it comes to the people we like, we believe we are gender-blind, but we are not so blind that we cannot see when things are uneven, unbalanced and unfair, often for both sexes.

In fact, when we look back over our lives we are astonished at our good fortune, growing up with feminism. Thanks to the confidence it gave us we have been more able to be true partners with the men in our lives, an achievement we believe has benefited both sides immeasurably. We were born at the right time. We understand that feminism is no magic bullet, and that it remains a work in progress, but we celebrate what feminism has done for us so far. And when we speak about this in public we receive an enthusiastic response, so it seems we're not the only ones who feel this way.

Such enthusiasm encouraged us to write this book, but the motivation primarily grew out of conversations over coffee for almost a decade. Together, after dropping our kids at school, we talked about what feminism meant to us and puzzled over why it was so disparaged. Now we've done it in writing.

Little did we realise what we were taking on. There have been knotty technical problems writing this book: in particular, the complexity of writing about the personal lives of two authors, while also examining how the times we lived through have affected our lives. In the end, to aid clarity and avoid as much confusion for the reader as we can, we have opted for writing about ourselves in the third person where we need to differentiate between each of the authors, and as 'we' elsewhere. We've also had to navigate our way through writing about various stages of feminism. Not as easy as it sounds, as there is a range of definitions. For our purposes, first-wave feminism is from the era of Mary Wollstonecraft – the late 18th century – through to the effort of the suffragettes in the early 20th to secure the vote. Second-wave feminism we define as the period from the 1960s to the 1980s when many of the legislative changes for equal rights were enacted. The latest incarnation of feminism is building on a third wave which draws attention to systemic barriers and attitudes that continue to hobble women's progress.

If you are hoping for a foolproof formula for how to live as a woman today, you won't find it here. We have struggled and fallen and made lots of mistakes. We cannot tell you how you should live your life. The most we can do is tell you how we have lived ours and what we have learnt along the way. We hope that this book will do for you what our conversations did for us: encourage you, amuse you, occasionally infuriate you and ultimately revitalise you.

The discussion of the feminist agenda has gone a bit quiet in recent years. While the idea of a little less conflict in our already busy and angst-ridden lives can be seductive, it is actually very dangerous. We can't stand still, because if feminism doesn't continue to move forward, progress won't simply plateau – it will go backwards. The conversation about women's role in society – however uncomfortable it may make many people feel – must reclaim its place as a serious and important issue. What follows is our attempt to kick-start that debate once again.

1

What do women want?

Women cop a barrage of criticism for just about any life decision they make these days. Stay-at-home mum? You're a lazy bludger wasting your education and turning into a boring housewife. Career woman? Ball-breaker with no social life. Working mother? Selfish, money-hungry cow who runs the distinct risk of bringing up juvenile delinquents. Part-time job? Not carrying your weight at work and probably taking a job from a full-time breadwinner. And so it goes on in the media, in political party rooms, workplaces, boardrooms, factory floors, extended family networks and cafés. Then there's been the outpouring of angst in books and articles from aggrieved childless working women; the statistics on the risks of childcare for the under-twos; the phenomenon of well-educated young women 'opting out' of their careers to become full-time mums, plus the endless bland corporate rhetoric about diversity and work/life balance.

Depending on who you're listening to, the great feminist revolution has either been so spectacularly successful there is no problem any more – women are equal and whatever they get or don't get is entirely their own responsibility – or has spectacularly failed because women were happier and more suited to being at home and minding the kids all along.

Amid this cacophony the two of us looked at each other and thought it was time to at least present another view. A perspective from women with reasonably satisfying jobs, more or less normal children (well they *are* teenagers) and apparently durable marriages. We wanted to explore the experience of women like us, in short. Women who have often been rendered silent by their status in society, the ridicule they attract from some quarters and their acceptance of the message that they have nothing of interest to say and no one would listen anyway.

To be fair, you couldn't shut us up if you tried, but that's not the point. For all our experience in media and communication we believe our voice, our views and the way we feel remain largely unrepresented. And here's the thing: it's still a man's world. The psychology of being a woman in a largely male-dominated world, we believe, should not only be more thoroughly explored but also considered from many different female points of view. It was what we did when we talked to each other and increasingly what we were being asked to share with others when we spoke at conferences and seminars. What had started as an informal collaboration we came to feel was worth setting out for a broader audience.

Every week for ten years (give or take the odd sick child, demanding boss and/or school function) we have met for coffee and unloaded about our usually hectic week as workers, voters, citizens, wives and most of all mothers. If we had believed everything we heard, and read, about women like us, we'd have thrown up our hands in despair years ago and retired hurt, but we didn't. Instead we looked around, at one another, at our friends, colleagues, neighbours and relatives and wondered just who the pundits were talking about.

No, we are not living the perfect lives — often quite the reverse. And we are not superwomen. (How that description became an insult is a book in itself!) The journey has been at times tiring and stressful. But has it been more interesting, satisfying and fulfilling than the lives our mothers led? We think so, and so do they. Our children seem to love us and have not yet ended up in the gutter. And our husbands are still around.

The double bind

For all these reasons and many more, we think it's time the hype and negativity about women's lives were carefully examined, along with the politics of the complex social changes that have occurred in our lifetimes. It is possible for women, particularly those with access to decent education, to have a rewarding life on many levels without giving away the chance of personal happiness. The personal is political, as the feminists of decades ago so famously contended. But while it may seem as though women are making myriad decisions about the way they want to live, actually their choices are still narrowed by a strong undercurrent of disapproval. In many ways, we believe the fact that more doors have opened has in itself made it harder to avoid this disapproval — a case of being damned if you do and damned if you don't. As conflicting opinion has increased about the different paths women have chosen, it's been hard for them to avoid absorbing this censure and many then punish themselves, through self-criticism and guilt.

It is obvious to us how this seeping sense of blame is manifesting in many parts of society. In the workplace, otherwise feisty women often stay silent in meetings or avoid starting discussions about their family life or interests with male bosses. As a columnist on these issues, Catherine has received hundreds of emails from outraged women who tell stories of men criticising women colleagues for talking to each other about kids and family in the office, only for them to launch into a lengthy dissection of the weekend's footy game with their male colleagues.

Double standards are alive and well and observable in social events through to board meetings. It's hard to believe in the early 21st century in Australia that it's still common at a party to see women sitting in one group and men in another. Or to go to an important business lunch and find major companies represented by several hundred men and a mere handful of women, usually seated together at a table in the back of the room. Women are silenced in more straightforward ways as well. Jane was part of a group of three businesswomen on a flight who were loudly shooshed by the female flight attendant during her safety demonstration. It is hard to imagine three businessmen being silenced in quite the same way. A small incident but indicative of the way women are routinely reminded of their lower status.

It's extraordinary how powerful the politics of gender can be and how effectively they stifle women. Not only are female opinions ignored, but women are also expected to shut up about their objections at being excluded from discussion. They are in a double bind. Speak up and women are tagged troublemakers; keep quiet and their needs are never registered and nothing changes. The muting of women in public domains, our research and experience tells us, is largely a result of them feeling powerless and scared. Fear is a daily adjunct for many women working in male-dominated organisations (and increasingly for men too, which shows how poorly our workplaces are at accommodating their employees full stop). The difference for women however is that their status is so routinely challenged and that they represent a tiny minority in the power groups in business, public and even community life. They are scared they will lose their jobs and will not be able to meet financial commitments; that they will not find another comparable position or have the wherewithal to fight their way through another hierarchy and 'earn' some flexibility; that they will be labelled a whinger or become an example of what the blokes knew all along: women shouldn't really be in the workplace. They are scared they will be called bad mothers or brainless housewives. They are scared of censure from men and women because in many places they are made to feel that they don't fit in. They are afraid they will be judged for their behaviour and found wanting, or that they are lacking femininity. And women like all human beings would rather align themselves with the powerful than the powerless.

We've seen all this and more in our lives, and watched in dismay the waste of talent and the increase in frustration in our community and among friends. It's a sad fact that progress for women in many parts of Australian society has been appallingly slow, but now it seems we are virtually going backwards. And if it's like this for two middle class, middle-aged, white Western women it's obviously much worse for those who struggle with low incomes and insecure jobs. Even for such relatively privileged women as ourselves paid work was never just a choice – it was a necessity. For women less financially secure than we are of course it has always been the norm – crucial for the family's survival. Given that reality, it is particularly cruel for society to overtly encourage women to take their place in the workforce and then covertly criticise them for being there. We believe our privilege has given us the means and the responsibility to air these issues so that conditions for all women, and therefore everyone else, improve.

Skim latte and flat white

During our years of friendship, one of us has lost both parents and the other has left three jobs and started two businesses. We have watched our children grow from biddable primary schoolers to rebellious and outspoken teenagers. We have struggled with marriage and emotional watersheds and made good and bad decisions just like everyone else. Consistently however, the encouragement – literally, the increase in courage – we have given one another has helped us through and become the major motivation behind this book.

Our honest, sometimes angry, often hilarious conversations have been rejuvenating. We have supported and inspired one another, exchanged ideas, opinions, whinges, worries, fears and grief. Yes, we cried as well as laughed and felt sick with doubt and at times with rage. But we worked something out.

Over the years (and the coffee – skim latte for Jane, flat white for Catherine) we've realised women not only absorb a lot of criticism, they are only too quick to castigate themselves. It turned out it wasn't just us. When we started talking with a range of women about writing this book, we were deluged with stories, anecdotes and – rather gratifyingly – support.

They like us have discovered that no matter which way you turn as a woman you trip over a set of expectations, rapidly followed by a mental calculation of how many times you have failed to match them. It's tiring and makes it difficult to keep a sense of proportion even when you have the means to know better. Sometimes we have simply realised we don't need to listen to those critical voices anymore because our lives have changed and age and experience have kicked in. But there have also been many dead ends we wished we had not gone down and plenty of angst and energy wasted which could have been avoided.

Our aim in this book is to help debunk much of the negative rubbish that is being thrown at women. It's also to explore why such opprobrium is continuing to emerge at a time of unprecedented economic prosperity, technological sophistication and opportunities for advancement. Many women we know are struggling to live their lives in an entirely new way, and it is wearing them out. By supporting one another, we have been able not only to find the spirit and energy to move forward, but most importantly to enjoy our lives and the freedom and confidence that comes from not expecting ourselves to be perfect or to have all the answers. We don't think it's a coincidence that as women make inroads in the workplace and public arenas the standards for child raising in middle-class circles keeps ratcheting up, and we'll be exploring this further in Chapter 8. Nor do we believe that much of the well-meaning but judgmental concern about the effects of childcare aimed fairly and squarely at their female parents is accidental either. Just add it to the list.

We both have extensive networks of female friends and colleagues and most of them are leading busy (OK, often too busy) lives, just like many of the men we know. But what worries us is the amount of their precious time and attention they invest in justifying their decisions in a way that men simply don't have to. It would never occur to most people to scrutinise a man's decision to combine raising a family with a paid job, for example. That's what men do − they go out and earn a living. Women have mortgages, rent, bills and superannuation costs; they have to earn a living too. Women have to be financially independent because many end up without a partner, widowed, divorced or simply without enough cash in retirement (more about that in Chapter 7). But women are still expected to participate in their community and in society in ways that men are not. Who usually fronts up to the school canteen, attends the P&C meeting and looks after aged parents? Who buys the Easter eggs, birthday presents, Christmas presents, not just for our immediate family but for everyone including teachers, children's friends and even the husband's relatives? Not to mention all the additional shopping, cooking and cleaning up that accompanies each and every one of those festivities.

Why us?

We have both been researching and discussing these issues for years. Jane has spent 30 years mixing it with the boys in one of the most male-dominated and competitive arenas in business: the advertising creative department. She has chalked up many 'firsts' when it comes to changing the perception of women in advertising: chairing prestigious award shows and helping to pioneer part-time work for creative people. With a weekly column, 'Corporate Woman', in a national newspaper to fill, Catherine has scoured the literature and kept up with the research, the latest books and articles, while interviewing scores of academics, authors, coaches and consultants, plus just about every senior executive woman in Australia at some time or another. And she's had a fair crack at interviewing many of our leading CEOs on these issues as well, and heard all about the latest 'diversity' policies from a phalanx of white, middle-aged men. But even with access to these incredible amounts of information and experience we've still found it difficult to recognise ourselves in any of this tidal wave of information.

We're sure we're not the only ones who feel like this. 'The market is wide open for a book on the real story of working women and how they rear their children'. (Deborah Hope, *The Australian*, 5 July 2006). That said, this is no voyage of self-discovery. We are not motivated just by a sense of inequity or because we are personally aggrieved – although we've been there. Our concern is that younger women than us are also being effectively gagged by the overwhelming sense they are at fault for any difficulties they encounter as they pursue a career, a role in public life, or simply raise issues that are specific to them. In fact, it has struck us that this stifling of women's voices for stepping out of line is becoming as effective at our end of the world as putting women in burkhas has become at the other (there's more about burkhas in Chapter 10). The most effective and profound example of this is that feminism has become the F word. To call yourself a feminist has become very risky.

Reaction to the F word has now reached such an extreme it is in danger of replacing misogyny. Where once some men could get away with voicing their dislike of women in general, now they target feminists (sometimes referred to as feminazis). Once again, women are forced to defend their human rights. The extreme misogyny expressed by some bloggers and forum-posters in the free-for-all that is the internet has brought us face to face with just how much some men (and some women) still hate and resent every small step towards freedom and respect women have taken.

We find this resentment particularly disturbing because between us we have five daughters (no sons). We would be appalled if they were so put off by this rhetoric they seriously considered either not having kids so they can build a career, or not having a career so they can have a family. Living less than a full life. What kind of life is it if you have to sacrifice a deep desire because of a lack of real options? We are wary of the use of the word choice in this context: what kind of 'choice' exists when you work punishingly long hours and are also expected to be chief homemaker and child-carer? Are these real choices in the true sense of the word? Yet many young women are being told that they have to make just such a 'choice' – that it's a personal issue for them to struggle with and resolve on their own.

This is not a scapegoating exercise – blaming men, career women or evil capitalist pigs for the dysfunction many women face at certain times in their lives. We have always believed a lot of the debate about who should shoulder the primary care giver's role seems ultimately insulting to fathers who are every bit as good as women at caring for kids – we've seen this with our own eyes. The debate about time, domestic and paid work and how to get the right mix is not solely a women's issue and we will never get anywhere while it is designated as such.

Feminism is about meeting these challenges by legitimising women's voices, experiences and feelings as they attempt to navigate such complexity. That's a tall order, and it's hardly begun. Given the relatively short time that female voices have been acknowledged in public life, we feel we're just at the cusp of change. It is a hopeful sign that for the first time in history, Australia has a female deputy prime minister, a female deputy opposition leader and seven women in the Cabinet. Things can change but, as we will see, they can change both for the better and the worse. Nevertheless, it seems the right moment to put some context around these matters and articulate how it feels to be born, as the old Chinese curse puts it, in such interesting times.

Feminism: a work in progress

A journalist friend of ours always says there are too many books in the world and not enough time to read them, so why write any more? But for us the overflow of information has given plenty of heat and not enough light. We want to scrutinise the system we live in, warts and all, and try to work out why a male breadwinner and dependent spouse model and the idea that housework is women's work have proved so hard to dismantle. Yes, the obvious answer is that no one wants to do the boring bits, but women have more bargaining power than they used to, so how come they (we) are still sorting out the socks? We're out and proud about hating housework (more on this in Chapter 5) and there's been a small shift in the dynamic in our homes. But for a lot of women it is still not acceptable to admit maintaining a sparkling and attractive home is a pain in the arse. And no matter how liberated we may claim to be, we remain acutely conscious that if the house is a mess, we're the ones who are judged. Our husbands may even be pitied!

Many of the women in our generation find it puzzling that feminism, which promised so much, appears to have stalled. It seemed so logical that, as night followed day, the education of women would mean their passage into all the realms where once only men had wielded power. It seems remarkably clueless now, but when we were hitting our twenties, we truly thought the battles would be long fought and won by the time we retired. What could hold us back if we had our degrees in one hand and a job contract in the other? Well, the rest, as they say, is history. Turns out quite a lot of things were hanging on our coat tails, and inevitably they included pots, brooms and babies, while up ahead was a glass ceiling protecting a steel floor. Or as US feminist Laura Liswood once said to Catherine, there's no such thing as the glass ceiling, just a thick layer of men.

Many of the obvious barriers that kept women penned in have started to dissolve. What hasn't disappeared are the attitudes and emotional reliance on the old ways of doing things, and the nostalgia for what some would argue was a simpler time and a more efficient division of labour. Change is painful, as all the management textbooks tell you, and the change in the status and role of women is one big change. Really big. It is, quite possibly, one of the greatest single revolutions in the history of humankind. After a lifetime as feminists we can now see that change of this magnitude was never going to happen either consistently or quickly.

No formula

A bit of real life experience goes a long way in this overwrought media age. It's also the way women exchange information. We tell stories, we confide, and sometimes it's disparaged as 'gossip'. But gossip is how we learn from one another, how we support one another and how we test out something new. As authors, we want to provide some role models that are about achievable lives – not extremes, or hard-to-relate-to generalisations. God knows there have been times we both would have loved to scurry home for a while and be cared for but we're here to tell you, the feeling passed. Spend a few hours with a screaming toddler and office politics takes on a rosy hue. Or we felt annoyed and angry about being overlooked again for a promotion and regretted moving to part-time work, until we got home and realised we needed those extra hours to sort out a homework crisis or arrange a birthday party. There are no easy formulae to follow here because women's lives and the demands they juggle are particularly messy. Many of us are making this up as we go along because we are the first generation to really try blending all these competing agendas.

If you steal a few hours to read this book here's what we hope you'll find: how a taste of education was an intoxicating, politicising and powerful incentive for our generation; how housework is boring and should be shared; how parenting standards are set too high and can be effectively lowered and still produce quality kids; how a job outside the house does not require offering up your first born but does need grim determination and a well-developed sense of the absurd; the effect of feminism on the developing world; how talking about feminism is like discussing al-Qaeda these days and why; how to let yourself off the hook, plus why feminists have better sex and a whole lot more. You may even find a laugh or two along the way.

Most of all we want to show you how we learnt to lighten up and cut ourselves some slack. And how that will help you achieve more than any desperate, self-punishing, approval-seeking behaviour ever could. Instead of shutting up about feminism, in fact, we feel like we've only just got started. We do hope what we are saying will come as a relief to all sorts of women, living all sorts of lives, who may also have been wondering when they were ever going to hear any good news about being a woman in today's society.

2

Learning to swear

We grew up in large families by today's standards in classic suburban bungalows surrounded by gum trees in northern Sydney nearly 50 years ago. In those days, dads had a job and mums looked after the house and kids, most of the time. But a change was coming.

We watched our mothers, our older sisters and our teachers change in front of our eyes. And the message they kept sending us was that the world was our oyster and that we had a right – even a duty – to do things differently, to develop our own potential, to refuse to put ourselves last. Essentially they were asking us to do what only young men had been asked to do in the past: to go out into the world and make something of ourselves. We were to be pioneers.

And, to a great extent, we have been. The world we left behind as children has gone – and gone forever. The majority of mothers and married women are now in paid employment, and feminism can claim some of the credit for this, but not all of it. The renewal of feminism in the 1970s was probably only possible because a whole range of factors came into play at the same moment. Despite the fact that many girls were not encouraged to continue their education, they were still more educated than they had ever been before. Also, as they do now, girls routinely outperformed boys at school, particularly in the humanities, and no society can afford to put money into educating half its population and then not use that resource. Meanwhile, the world of work was changing too. It was on the brink of the great technological revolution that was to see a rapid decrease in traditional physical, usually male, occupations and a rapid increase in highly skilled, office-based occupations. The market economy needed to bring its women into the workplace and so they came.

Timing is everything

Meanwhile, our own decisions about our lives were as much the result of good luck as good management. We are deeply grateful to have been born where and when we were, with the privilege of middle-class security and exquisite timing. Doors were opening for us. Our families also provided us with some strong role models. Does having a group of feisty female relatives around you make a difference to how a young girl looks at life? We both believe it had a major impact on us, and our view of the world. We may not have been raised by placard-waving feminists (although Jane's mother Kate has joined a picket line or two) but our mothers were uncompromising and outspoken women. They were both frustrated by their lack of access to formal education and they made it clear they didn't want us to live with those regrets. We owe them a lot.

Our mothers were not alone in their frustration. A prominent public figure, renowned for his conservative views, told Jane about his unsatisfying relationship with his mother. He loved both his parents, he said, but he only really *liked* his father. In his view, the trouble was simply that mothers are controlling of their sons, wanting to live through them, in effect. To this conservative man, this seemed just a fact of life, until Jane pointed out this situation wasn't intrinsic to mothers and sons, but simply what happened when intelligent and energetic women were given no other outlet than living through their children − particularly their male children. 'That is another gift feminism has given us,' she couldn't resist telling him, 'the ability of women to live their own lives, and so be less controlling of their children.'

Catherine grew up in a secure middle-class home, the second of four children. Her mother Patricia did not work outside the home although she was often out and about, visiting relatives and friends all over Sydney and working in a variety of voluntary jobs. Not all latchkey children have parents in the workforce, as Catherine and her siblings discovered, often arriving home from school with instructions to find the spare key and get themselves sorted out. Although it was a traditional family in many ways, Patricia consistently encouraged her daughters, as well as her sons, to aim for a university education and a career. Her father John also made it clear he expected the same from his girls as his boys. It was not an expectation shared by the parents of most of her friends and it had an enormous impact on Catherine's assumptions, expectations and decisions.

Coming from staunchly Catholic stock, Catherine was educated by nuns from the local convent and from Grade 3 her school was single sex. Her high school was relatively small, and there were no grand vision statements or exhortations to go forth and conquer the world. Many of her classmates left in Year 10 to join the workforce. With virtually no career guidance on offer and relatively modest expectations from the school – and society – most of her Year 12 class did not go on to university. Some 30 years later, at a reunion, a couple of them told Catherine they deeply regretted these choices and some had returned to study in later life. But it was hardly surprising there were few expectations – young women were only starting to understand the options opening up before them and were mostly unprepared for the continuing cultural and social resistance to their progress.

Like most kids in those days – particularly those in large families – Catherine certainly did not experience the anxious helicopter parenting that seems de rigeur now. Far from being hot-housed children were usually meant to be seen and not heard in those days. You got on with your homework or not, but your parents rarely checked. Exams and assignments were your call, although both parents were happy to help if needed. On HSC results day, Catherine's parents were overseas, and she waited until they were back a few days later to let them know her results – inconceivable now.

Not that her parents were particularly laid back or easygoing types. It was a conservative home in many ways and the breadwinner was head of the household. The fact that there was one income meant budgets were tight even on a professional's salary. Unusually, Patricia had some income of her own, and it made quite a difference to the family – a fact not wasted on Catherine.

Meanwhile, just a few suburbs away in Sydney's north, the Caro family was similarly unconventional. A friend from a much more traditional background who met Jane when they were both 14 remembered the household dynamics.

> I used to love going to stay at Jane's house. Unlike my home, the TV was on 24/7, we ate when we liked and stayed up all night if we wished. Jane's dad was always downstairs with the TV on sport, volume at full blast, reading glasses half way down his nose, sound asleep in a reclining chair. Jane's mum was always out and no one seemed to know where. This intrigued me coming from a home where my mother was always in the kitchen. I was also asked to call them both by their first names, which seemed so radical. The Caros' house was always full of people's voices yelling passionately about something to each other from various rooms in the large house. I was in awe of it all. (Sally Yuncken, in conversation, 20 October 2007)

Unlike Catherine, Jane was raised in a family without religious beliefs. Her mother Kate was a lapsed Methodist to the extent that she could more fairly be described as anti-Methodist and was uncompromising in her atheism. Her father, Andy, identified as an agnostic and was unaware of any religious tradition in his family of origin. There is some evidence that his family was originally Jewish. She was sent to the local co-ed, comprehensive public school for all 13 years of her school life and received an excellent education. It is to this coeducational schooling that she credits her ability to mix it successfully in the boy's playground that is the advertising creative department. Despite her often radical politics, like Catherine's mother Patricia, Kate did not go out to paid work while her children were young, but as Jane grew into adolescence, she did become very active in various causes and crusades. An early environmentalist, she fought the attempt to put an airport in Duffy's Forest and won. As a feminist, she joined the Women's Electoral Lobby and led the Liberal Feminist Network. As a result, she was often not at home and when she was, her children found her invariably on the phone.

Typically for his generation, Andy worked hard to climb the corporate ladder, which he did very successfully. This took a great deal of his time and energy. Family meals were reserved for Sunday nights, otherwise Kate and the kids ate together and Andy had something on toast when he came home. Nevertheless, he was a loving and engaged husband and father. Jane credits her excellent spelling to the relentless spelling challenges he set for his children as they ate dinner together every Sunday. Most importantly of all, Andy always gave Jane the impression that he believed there was nothing she could not do and nothing she could not achieve. There is a great deal of angst about the relationship between fathers and sons at the moment, but not enough attention is paid to the equally vital relationship between fathers and daughters. It is a girl's father, we believe, who gives her the confidence she needs to brave the public sphere, and we are both eternally grateful to our own fathers for that.

Taking over the quadrangle

Jane was the first woman in her family to go to university (but certainly not the last). So revolutionary were the 1970s however that somewhat to Jane's chagrin, her mother went to university at the same time. Campuses after 1972, thanks to the new Whitlam government abolishing university fees, were crawling with middle-aged women eager to make up for lost opportunities. The response of younger undergraduates at the time was mixed, particularly, it must be said, among some of the male students. Not only were these women bright and experienced, they were highly motivated and studied hard. Suddenly a group of young men not only were having to get used to competing with more women than they ever had before, they had to deal with being bested by them. And not just any women either, but often by women who reminded them of their mothers!

Jane remembers being in an English Literature tutorial with five mature-aged (as they were euphemistically called) women students and one young man of about her own age. The tutor was male, and an outspoken gay activist. The young man was in the middle of presenting his first paper when he basically had a meltdown, verbally attacking the women in the room for giving him a hard time, even though not one of them had spoken a word. The tutorial changed from a discussion of Victorian novels to a group counselling session where this young man (who had no sisters and had attended an all-boys school) was kindly and wisely put back together again by the motherly women in the room. So skilled were they, he remained in the tutorial and eventually became a good friend to the women.

A woman who returned to uni in the ACT at this time as a mature-aged student to gain a degree in education remembers being irritated by a textbook on adolescent psychology. It stated that there was no greater hormonal disruption than adolescence. In her view, as the mother of four, the hormonal changes in adolescence simply did not compare with those experienced by women during pregnancy and lactation and she did not hesitate to point this out. The lecturer was nonplussed, and a vigorous debate broke out, with many women agreeing with her. Eventually a male student could stand it no longer. Red-faced with fury, he demanded of the lecturer; 'How long are you going to allow this woman to contradict the textbook?'

For the first time, females and female experience were entering public spaces and demanding to be taken not just into account but seriously. This was the heady and exhilarating atmosphere in which young women of our generation were educated. Even the returned servicemen who surged into university after WWII, changing forever the cosy, upper-class, born-to-rule mentality of those hallowed halls, did not cause the same pitch of emotion created when women invaded higher education.

If asked at the time we went to uni, we would probably have said our ambitions were modest, and marriage and family, if we thought of them at all, were somewhere in the future. We both felt uncomfortable with the idea of teaching or nursing but at least there were now other options, thanks to feminism. And we felt lucky to have them. We were confident the world was transforming in a way the previous generation found extraordinary. By the time we left university in the 1970s there was a sense among our peer group that women had much the same choices as men. Sure, there was plenty of progress to be made. But a whole generation of young women were emerging from higher education armed with degrees their mothers could never have dreamed of attaining (at the same youthful age, anyway). They were exciting times.

Out into the cold

We believed nothing would hold us back. For women of our generation there was a strongly-held belief that the process that began with access to education, and gained momentum by allowing us to control our fertility, would obviously continue to fall into place as we entered the workforce. As we sailed out of study and into the office it was with high hopes of long and successful careers that matched it with the boys we knew. After all, we'd pretty easily matched it with them in education. They just didn't seem that bright or formidable to us. If we'd beaten them in school and at uni, why couldn't we outperform them at work?

And it wasn't that hard getting a job. We left uni in times of high employment, and university degrees were still rare, with about ten per cent of the school population going on to higher education. (These days, it's around three times that number.) We were in demand, but we were already starting to receive some warning signals about what lay ahead. One of the major barriers we certainly hadn't anticipated in workplaces was the resistance of other women. Jane remembers being employed as a junior product manager at a major multi-national company, the first woman to hold such a post in the very conservative − and oddly male − world of laundry detergent manufacturing. Those were the days when women did the buying and consuming and men did the making and selling. When she was told her application for the position had been successful, she was also sternly warned that one person strongly objected to her getting the job. 'This person is much more important to us than you are,' she was told, 'so it is your job to win her over.' The person who so strongly objected to having a woman in a management position (albeit the most junior such position imaginable) was the CEO's secretary.

And Jane did win her over, always saying please and thank you whenever she needed to ask her to do anything, making her coffee and helping her with the photocopying and filing. None of the other trainee product managers were expected to behave in such a manner, because they were all male. Women were used to working for men at the time but were deeply uncomfortable about working for women. Treating clerical staff with courtesy and respect was a valuable lesson and has paid off in spades ever since, but at the time, Jane knew she had no option. She either placated the secretary or risked losing her job.

Despite such small hiccups, we remained optimistic. Sure, there would be teething problems. When we looked up at all the people above us in our workplaces, there wasn't a woman among them. We knew change was painful, we expected to meet some resistance, but we had brains and degrees and right on our side (famous last words). The women we did see in the workplace mostly worked as clerks — this was before computers had taken over data processing — and were no advertisement for working after marriage and kids. After punching an adding machine all morning, these women flew into the city at lunchtime to buy the groceries for that night's evening meal, then left their desks on the dot of 5 pm to commute back to the suburbs to prepare tea for their husband and children.

For women of our age, however, the gates were opening. In her first year working for the laundry detergent company, Jane attended an annual in-house management training course. At the end of the course, the trainer confided that after 15 years of running the same program, this was the first year in which half the participants were women. Prior to that, he told her, there had been one or two female trainees at best.

Focused as we were on doing well in our workplaces and impressing our bosses, we didn't think much about how we'd handle that pressure if one day we got married and had kids. Maybe that would happen, but not yet. And when it did, surely the blokes would come to the party and help out? If a woman pulls in a wage then it's only fair to share the domestic load too, we thought. That way the responsibility can be shared just like the financial load.

Even by the time we eventually became 'working mothers' our views, while more pragmatic, remained optimistic. Childcare options were limited when our kids were born, 20 years ago. But again, we couldn't imagine it would always be the case as the mass movement of women into jobs continued. Our kids seemed to enjoy childcare and were only there for a few days a week. Surely the provision of caring centres and other options such as family day care would burgeon as demand increased?

How wrong − and naive − it all sounds now. The wave of younger women entering paid work has certainly continued its upward swing but there's been less change in workplaces than we hoped for all those years ago, particularly for mothers. In fact, Australia has a dubious distinction in this regard.

> While there has been an increase in the proportion
> of women with dependent children entering the labour
> market, Australia compares unfavourably with other
> OECD countries. Although the employment rate declines
> for women with children in all other countries, Australia
> is noteworthy for the steepness of this decline. While
> the decline in participation is substantial for women
> with one child, it is among the most extreme of 23
> OECD countries for women with two or more children.
> This suggests that motherhood has a more detrimental
> impact on women's labour force participation in Australia
> than in most other countries. ('Women's Lifework: Labour
> market transition experiences of women', Ciara Smyth,
> Margot Rawsthorne and Peter Siminski, Social Policy
> Research Centre, August 2005)

This 'motherhood impact' has contributed to the snail's pace of change in many Australian workplaces, despite our hopes and the rhetoric about a new world of work. Even minor 'concessions' (and that's how they are described) such as paid maternity leave in some companies or flexible hours, have not had much impact on the trenchant views about who bears the responsibility of home and kids. Contrary to our naive and youthful expectations, stereotypes about gender are alive and kicking (see Chapter 6). Nevertheless, something fundamental was altering. The feminist revolution that helped open up education and the workplace to the second sex gained another significant boost thanks to the world of medical research. As we were growing up and studying in high school the contraceptive pill became widely available.

The sexual revolution

It is revealing of the mores of the time that the pill's developers originally envisaged it to be used by married women to help them space their families and so protect their health. They could never have imagined the sexual revolution their efficient and effective method of female-controlled contraception would unleash. If they had, perhaps they would never have gone through with it. Indeed, whenever anyone asks what the most revolutionary inventions of the last century were, while others cite the internal combustion engine or nuclear fusion, we always silently toss up between the tampon and the contraceptive pill. We simply can't imagine what our lives would have been like without either of them.

Control over fertility is fundamental for women's quest for equity and basic human rights. The pill's ability to unshackle women from their fertility changed the very notion of the role of women in society. But it did not instantly address all those complicated issues around sex, childbearing and gender. Again, looking back, we thought access to oral contraception would be accompanied by cultural change and new gender roles. Women could have different partners and not run the risk of falling pregnant. It seemed at last women would have the same liberty in their sexual lives as men had enjoyed for centuries.

Yes, it seems ludicrous today to think that a small white pill could bear the burden of so many expectations. But it was miraculous to us – cheap, accessible and fairly risk free. However, it appalled many on the religious right and unleashed a wave of hysteria about its effect on morality in general and that of young women in particular. Even as teenagers we found the hypocrisy around sexual behaviour shocking. A well-meaning priest once told Catherine's religion class that he'd heard every silly excuse from teenage girls who had wound up pregnant. No mention of the boys – maybe they weren't asked ...

Nevertheless, there was a new liberalism everywhere. Jane moved in with her boyfriend (now husband of 32 years) in 1975 when she was not quite 19. In those days it was still routinely referred to as 'living in sin'. Always ahead of their time, her parents subsidised her income because as a uni student her part-time work did not bring in the wage that her full-time working boyfriend was able to earn. As a good feminist, Jane's mother described the subsidy as the means to ensure her eldest daughter retained her economic independence. Jane was also asked to debate the ethics of her lifestyle with a priest in front of the student body at a local Catholic boys' school, and despite some trepidation, was surprised by the courtesy and respect with which both she and her lifestyle were treated by all concerned. The boys, perhaps not so surprisingly, voted unanimously to award the debate in her favour.

Not everyone was so sanguine, however. The heat generated by living arrangements that are now so routine as to be unremarkable was disproportionate. When Jane was accidentally locked out from the house she shared with her boyfriend and other flatmates, the carer of their elderly landlady next door not only refused to give her the spare key but refused even to address a word to her. It was a novel – and not entirely unpleasant experience – to be treated as a scarlet woman. Interestingly, once the elderly landlady herself discovered what was going on, she hurriedly – and very sweetly – hobbled over offering both the key and profuse apologies.

Unexpected consequences

The huge change that accompanied second-wave feminism was the breaking down of the taboo around sexual freedom and sexual enjoyment for women. The female orgasm, it is said, was invented in 1968. At the same time, the pill opened up more than a new and freer attitude to sexual morality. It did what it was designed to do – allowed women to postpone or plan childbearing. While this seemed like nothing but a blessing at the time, over the longer term it has brought a range of other dilemmas. Now we regularly hear about the despair of older women who left their run to motherhood too late.

However, young women – including our daughters – couldn't imagine a world where relatively safe and accessible contraception isn't available. Not that young people are in such a hurry to move out on their own any more. Perhaps directly due to the entrenched liberality of their parents, cohabiting with boyfriends and girlfriends beneath the parents' roof is now very much accepted. Unlike the US and despite the emergence of evangelical Christian movements like Hillsong and their particular appeal to those under 30, the campaign to persuade young people to remain virgins until marriage doesn't seem to be catching on very strongly in this country.

Yet the confusion and angst over sexuality and how it is

expressed by women and men is just as fraught as ever. In fact, the ripples from the introduction of that innocuous little pill and its progeny – the morning after pill and RU486 (see Chapter 3) – continue to upset many. It would have been impossible to anticipate, for example, that a few decades on the rise of raunch culture (see Chapter 11) would see young, well-educated women happily stripping off to pole dance in front of their male friends.

We weren't doing that kind of thing at uni, although we had our fair share of good times with our friends – and Jane does remember wearing a very skimpy costume on stage as the Queen of Sodom and Gomorrah in a skit in a university revue. But in our early twenties, clutching our bright shiny degrees, it was the world of work and achievement that interested us. As for our personal lives – marriage, children, domesticity – once considered the all-consuming interest of the female gender, Jane, although she didn't know it yet, was already in the relationship that would lead her to marriage. And Catherine was not even thinking about walking up the aisle.

Neither of us would have predicted we'd end up in the 'burbs with kids a few decades on. Nor would we have imagined that it would be the experiences of mothering and housekeeping that would radicalise our commitment to feminism far more than the workplace ever would.

3

The shock of the real world

As we emerged bright-eyed and bushy-tailed into the adult world of work and family, we believed the good fight for gender equity would be done and dusted by the time our own children were reaching adulthood. As you are about to see, we couldn't have been further off the mark. We need to take a clear-eyed look at what tripped us up, however, so we can help those following us to understand and therefore avoid the same obstacles.

A couple of years ago, Jane was invited to speak about her experiences of 25 years of writing ads at a course for fledgling copywriters. She finished her speech, answered a few questions, gathered her notes and prepared to leave. As she was walking out the door, a young woman detached herself from the crowd. 'I didn't want to ask you this during general question time,' she said, 'because it's off the topic, but you are the only female copywriter we've heard about who has managed to combine a successful career with a family. How did you do it?'

As middle-aged mums with careers, we get asked this often,

usually by apologetic and slightly embarrassed young women who obviously feel they are intruding on something that is 'personal', and so out of bounds. Far from feeling put upon by such questions, however, it seems to us that these are the most important ones we are ever asked. It's such a relief to escape the slightly phoney world of the unrelentingly 'professional' and get a chance to talk about what really interests us – life.

We recognise that it was never our lack of professional skills that got in our way as we moved through the world of work. It was always when we tried to live a whole life that we tripped over previously invisible stumbling blocks. At an annual newspaper advertising conference, The Caxtons, a few years ago one of the very few female creative directors in the business gave a speech about a typical day in her life. It started at 7 am and ended long past 8 pm. Early that morning one of her staff, a young female copywriter, popped into her office. Without preamble, she blurted out that she was pregnant, then burst into tears. When the creative director asked why she was crying, the young woman confessed she was terrified that her pregnancy would mean she'd lose her job and destroy her career. Reassured on that front by her boss, the young woman left, drying her eyes. The creative director then told the audience that her staff member was 34, exactly the same age as she was, and that there was absolutely no way she could fit a baby into her own highly demanding job. She knew the copywriter could probably juggle a job and a baby, but in her own case as a senior manager, she realised that by following her ambitions she was sacrificing her chances of ever having a child.

Young women may be loath to admit it, but many of them as they forge ahead in the world of work, enjoying its undoubted rewards – money, social life, stimulation and status – worry about what they will do if they have a baby. More and more, it seems to us, they feel they have an either/or choice.

The discussion that followed the creative director's speech at The Caxtons gives us some clues as to why this may be. Some women in the audience pointed out that workplaces which actually discourage women from having children were counterproductive to everyone's objectives, but particularly those of business. This attitude will eventually cut both the supply and demand end of the economic equation, because if the birth rate falls there will be fewer potential employees and customers. This was comprehensively pooh-poohed by most of the men in the room, particularly those on the panel. A woman's decision to have a child, it was roundly declared, was her own and nothing to do with business or employers. Someone even called it a 'lifestyle choice'. Those who attempted to refute this were both bullied and ridiculed, with the usual result of shutting down opposition. It was clear the subject made people uncomfortable and was not to be talked about. The young women in the room were left in little doubt: if you want to have a baby, you are on your own.

As a result of countless incidents like this, many women now believe the corporate doors are open for only a certain type of female – those who could be called 'men in skirts'. The covert message seems to be that if you want to compete on your merits in a man's world, so be it, but you will have to do it just as a man does. The women who get ahead are either exceptional, the story goes, have an exceptional boss, or manage to compartmentalise their personal life from their work life just as men have been taught to do. There has been progress in the world of paid work, but it makes little allowance for the realities of women's lives.

This apparently insoluble conundrum, reeking of biological determinism, has helped to reinforce the current 'feminism has failed' mantra. It seems illogical to us to blame feminism for failing women, however, for what is a lack of social justice – particularly as the movement has really just begun to gather pace after centuries of patriarchy. On the contrary, feminism gave us the confidence to take our talents and use them in interesting and stimulating careers, in work that paid us a decent amount of money, which in turn gave us a sense of independence and mastery over our own fates. Despite the many difficulties each of us has faced, we wouldn't want to have been born female at any other time in history.

But, to return to the question that opened this chapter, when we are asked how we did it, we cannot offer any foolproof formulas. Instead, we usually smile ruefully and share a few of our own more disastrous stories about how we muddled through. A tactic that did help was the realisation we needed to sit down and reassess what success meant to us – on every level. And we discovered that it was the ability to give ourselves some credit for whatever it was we'd achieved, large or small, that made us feel successful. It wasn't how other people judged us that mattered most; it was the kind of judgment we passed on ourselves. We became 'successful' once we'd learnt to stop castigating ourselves for not living up to other people's expectations – well, some of the time, anyway. And isn't that what feminism's about? Women having the courage to defy expectations and create a path that's meaningful for them?

Turning the corner

The achievements of feminism today of course are not just observed in the world of paid work. Most importantly there has been a massive shift around the fundamental respect shown towards women as human beings (with some notable exceptions). To understand better women's status today we often think back to our early teens and the casual sexism that surrounded us.

Back in the 1970s, Jane still recalls the brother of a friend telling her that women were simply not as intelligent as men, a belief that was still commonly held. She remembers bright female students weeping bitterly when forced to leave school after Year 10, usually by their fathers, while their less academically inclined brothers stayed on. Girls did not need a good education, many still believed, because their destiny was to marry and have children. Around the same period, a senior university academic we know who happened to be female wanted to buy a unit in Elizabeth Bay, but the bank would not lend her money without a male guarantor. Not being married, she eventually managed to obtain a shaky signature from her elderly father who had Alzheimer's disease, and was given the loan.

Such intrinsic insults and demeaning attitudes were considered entirely reasonable and normal only a few decades ago. But they are hard to credit now. No wonder it is often so difficult to convince people born into the so-called 'post-feminist era' that up until the early 1970s, women were routinely and overtly belittled, disregarded and legally discriminated against. We saw hard evidence of this generational divide recently. A couple of years ago the ABC revisited old episodes of 'A Big Country' to see what had changed. Many were fascinating, but there was one that stood out, which looked at the CWA (Country Women's Association). The commentary from the old 1960s program by a male reporter was most extraordinary. The cosy but utterly contemptuous tone he used about these earnest, serious and intelligent women was gobsmacking. How could we not have heard such things at the time, and how completely insulting it was to talk this way? Yet such a patronising tone was invisible back then, because it was so common. We all, women and men, were used to it and accepted it as normal. The insult registered, but it was not consciously acknowledged and therefore did more harm than a direct assault. Those women probably felt humiliated, but blamed it on their own stupidity, their own femaleness.

But this second-class citizen treatment was starting to produce a reaction. A growing awareness of sexist behaviour was reflected in popular culture as well. On 17 April 2007 The Biography Channel broadcast a program on the history of the top-rating American CBS program 'The Mary Tyler Moore Show'. The documentary gave a fascinating perspective on how far women have come. Premiering in 1970, 'The Mary Tyler Moore Show' was the first US sitcom to feature a 30-year-old single career woman. Originally, the writers of the series wanted Mary's character (Mary Richards) to be newly divorced, but – back in the 1970s – this was simply unacceptable to station executives and so Mary became merely single. Indeed, CBS executives so disliked the entire concept of the show, that it was only produced because the network was locked into a contract. It was expected to be a failure and condemned to a graveyard timeslot.

The show went on to become one of the most awarded,

watched and loved sitcoms in American television history, running continuously until 1977. During that time, Mary Richards broke much new ground in the way women were portrayed. Mary was gradually and cautiously allowed a sex life, although she never had a steady boyfriend. The writers toyed with the idea of having Mary and her boss Lou Grant fall into each others arms at the end of the last show, but resisted the temptation. Over the years, many new perspectives on women, life and work were aired. In one particularly resonant episode Mary confronted Mr Grant about why her predecessor as Associate Producer of the News had been paid $50 a week more than her.

'Because he was a man,' replies Lou Grant blithely (so unacceptable had voicing such a belief already become that the studio audience burst into loud and shocked laughter). Mary protests, arguing that she does the same work and does it just as well. 'Better,' interrupts Mr Grant, leaving her spluttering at the unfairness. He then elaborates. 'But it is fair, you are a single women and he was a married man with three children.' This male-breadwinner argument was often used at the time by those defending higher wages for men. Noticing that Mary has been rendered speechless by his argument, Mr Grant presses home his advantage and tells Mary that until she can think of an answer to that one, she should not come back into his office. Mary gets up and leaves the room, only to reappear a moment later. Forcefully she explains that such justifications are spurious and have nothing to do with her situation. 'You'd have to pay a man with three children more money than a man with two children, if that was really the case,' she says. 'And you don't.'

These were the arguments that were going on heatedly in

homes and offices and workplaces all over the developed world in this period, but they are not often heard any more. However, before getting too self-congratulatory, it's clear that, while such views may have been silenced, the continuing disparity between male and female pay shows the circumstances they reflected still remain. Whereas once Grant's views were acceptable, now they have been driven underground. Watching 'The Mary Tyler Moore Show' 30 years on is a potent reminder of how women were regarded when second-wave feminism began. That the issues the show highlighted have not been resolved is as good a reason as any for the conversation to continue, repeatedly and vigorously.

Unforeseen obstacles

Such was the logic and hope that accompanied feminism's beginnings, so powerful and rapid was its initial impact, that it is possible we all came to expect far too much of it. We watched smug, badly-thought out sexism, like that of Lou Grant, topple and thought that all barriers would fall as easily. Some even argued that sexism would disappear forever once the older generation had died out. Such commentators underestimated the size and nature of the barriers they faced as, no doubt, did we. What perhaps we failed to understand back then was that the most stubborn barrier to women's progress was not education, or being taken seriously. It was, simply, who changes the nappies, cooks the meals and cleans the loo.

Even armed with a phalanx of university degrees and advanced qualifications the workplace remains a formidable frontier for women (more of this in Chapter 6). And at home the balance has hardly shifted. Women still do around 80 per cent of home chores and caring tasks, despite their increasing workforce participation. The importance of this enduring housework burden can't be underestimated. In fact, those who dismiss the housework debate as peripheral are usually those who don't have to do any chores – to them the work is actually and metaphorically invisible (see Chapter 5). Many analysts in this area have pointed out that by burdening women with the psychological and physical responsibility for chores and children they are then locked into an endless cycle of taking lower-paid, more flexible jobs, jettisoning career or promotion prospects and reinforcing the stereotype that women are really not suited to using their brains. Not to mention increasing the already corrosive guilt working women feel about not being a good enough homekeeper and mother.

There are many reasons women fail to break through the ranks or access better-paid work, not least the difficulty in combining childbearing with peak career years at the office or workplace. But there's more to it than that. The culture in many workplaces continues to marginalise women, no matter how talented or unencumbered with family responsibilities they may be. With hindsight, it's abundantly obvious our expectations about the speed of progress as we left school or university were not realistic and in fact were not even taking into account a whole array of interrelated impediments.

At its most visible, the impact of these barriers shows up in the latest research and data about women in the workforce. Women are disproportionately represented in low-paid and casual jobs in Australia. At the other end of the spectrum, the picture is also bleak. Every two years a major report on the number of women in executive and director roles in Australia's business community is published by the Equal Opportunity for Women in the Workplace Agency (EOWA). This census tracks the progress or otherwise of women in shattering the glass ceiling.

The data has been collected for years, and its release is accompanied by a regular barrage of official commentary from EOWA and prominent business women, all expressing their confidence the figures are heading in the right direction. If the hoopla is a little bit strained, by and large the official optimism about the data usually seems justified. Until 2006. The census report released in late August of that year was a real problem to talk up. The statistics were not just poor; they revealed a slide backwards. A mere five women were CEOs of the ASX top 200 companies, and only three women chaired companies. Just over 12 per cent of executive managers were women and 8 per cent were board directors. Not only are Australian businesses failing to promote and appoint women, as a nation we are falling well behind comparable economies such as Canada and South Africa (EOWA, Australian Census of Women in Leadership 2006).

Anna McPhee, executive director of EOWA, dubbed the rate of progress 'glacial'. Yep, we are in an ice age. The census figures are part of a pattern of evidence that shows women are not achieving the goals once thought to require just a bit more time and some extra education. It was a message repeated often as we were making our way through jobs and careers. Keep working hard and playing by the rules, we were told, and we'd take over the world.

The blocked pipeline

Every prediction when we were students or just starting out in the workplace seemed to come to the same conclusion – it would just take time. The pipeline theory was understood by most women. According to this idea, it would simply be a matter of reaching a critical mass of women in the office or workplace and then the shift into senior ranks or non-traditional occupations would gradually happen. More women would emerge as managers or as miners, electricians and factory supervisors alongside their male colleagues. This explanation was so popular and seemingly inevitable it may well have lulled a cohort of feminists into a false sense of security. Catherine can remember being told on numerous occasions to relax and get on with the job because all would be well. By default, the unfairness of conditions would magically disappear. At home, it went without saying, the same metamorphosis would also transform gender roles. It wouldn't be easy but somehow we would all pitch in and manage. We even thought blokes would happily see the logic in this (OK, we were young).

That famous pipeline remained blocked partly because of stereotypes about what women could and should do. The power of this gender role bias is that it isn't simply imposed on women; it has been absorbed by them. Women are constrained by prejudices around their capabilities and social expectations, while men struggle to see their female colleagues as serious players in the workplace. Another cliché – the glass ceiling – was then coined to explain why women could get to a certain point in the workplace, but no further. But, of course, women in the workplace were dealing with a double whammy. While they battled with themselves and their male competitors in the office, they still carried the burden of traditional women's work at home.

The classic sequestration of women in the home toiling in unpaid work may have been unfair but it was efficient and unchallenged for centuries – until modern capitalism called on the troops from the suburbs to bolster the world of commerce, of course. That call to arms conveniently ignored the home. However, feminism, contrary to the popular belief today, never devalued labour in the private sphere. How could it, when domestic labour was not regarded as having any value in the first place? Housework and childcare, however necessary, has never been high status work – not in any society. High status women historically outsourced the care of the house and children and that defined their class. The Victorian ideal of the 'angel of the house' in reality had a very uneasy position in society.

Nonetheless, while the workplace pipeline remains stubbornly blocked and women still carry the majority of the domestic burden, progress has been made. Feminism has done more than help women who are entering the workforce to recognise the inequity they face and to object to it. It has revealed that obstacles like the glass ceiling will not disappear of their own accord. Women will have to get their hands dirty and dismantle them for themselves.

As we earned our first full-time wages, it never occurred to us that workplace barriers would prove so stubborn, especially as other significant obstacles had been spectacularly diminished. Indeed, as we were maturing from girls to women, the change in the roles expected of us was given much-needed impetus by circumstances quite separate from concerns about equity or social justice.

Sexual politics

The advent of cheap and effective contraception did change the relationship between gender and power, although not without a fight, and the freedom to plan a family is a significant advantage for women. But even this giant step forward has brought with it a new set of dilemmas. Although women now have more power over their bodies, many now tussle with their biological clocks, jobs and motherhood. And abortion remains a hot political topic. The recent parliamentary debate over the so-called 'abortion pill' stands as a vivid example of this.

The debate over the introduction of RU486 was remarkable for the way it split men and women, particularly in the Senate. All but three of the 28 female senators, no matter which party they belonged to, voted in favour of the amendment – female solidarity in anyone's language. The male senators, however, were evenly divided – 22 voting with the majority of women, and 25 voting against them. The result reveals there are issues in our community that unite women regardless of political persuasion. Women's lives, particularly their reproductive lives, are theoretical to men, but are stark reality to us.

During the debate, Senator Amanda Vanstone (Liberal) was particularly effective as she saltily pointed out to 'the boys' in the Upper House that it was easy for them to object to this bill. Senator Lyn Allison (Democrat) called the pious lecturing by some of the male senators 'galling', as women around Australia nodded their heads. And Julia Gillard (Labor) told then Health Minister Tony Abbott, 'For God's sake, Tony, it's not about you.'

Yet today's discussions around abortion have not progressed

as far as we hoped. We find it offensive when we hear men and some women objecting to women terminating pregnancy on what they call 'lifestyle' grounds, as if choosing to go ahead with a pregnancy is like deciding whether to buy a new handbag. The lifestyle grounds they sneer at may well involve a woman thinking seriously about what kind of a parent she is likely to be and her ability to commit fully to the child she may bring into the world, particularly if she's poor, under-age and single.

Compulsory parenthood has always been a recipe for disaster. Indeed, the best-selling book *Freakonomics* claims that 18 years after the Roe v Wade case in the US Supreme Court legitimised abortion in America, crime rates in the US began to fall. Doubting their own data, the authors of the book explored other possible explanations until they realised that the five US States that had undertaken abortion law reform two years prior to Roe v Wade also experienced drops in crime rates two years before the rest of the country, presumably because poorer women were able to end unwanted pregnancies (Levitt & Dubner 2005). Bad and reluctant parenting, it seems, can be much worse than not parenting.

Women, who still do the heavy lifting when it comes to parenting, are much more conscious of the huge responsibility it is to bring a child into the world – and the enormous commitment and effort that is required to *bring them up well*. Most of us, as demonstrated by the female senators, would rather a child had a right to a decent life than just a right to life. And this gender divide is not just obvious in Australia. In the US, both George Bush senior and junior are anti-abortion, while both their wives, Barbara and Laura, are pro-choice. Even Bush's Secretary of State

Condoleezza Rice describes herself as 'mildly' pro-choice ('Women Closest to Bush are Pro-Choice', Ann Gerhart, <Washingtonpost.com>, 19 July 2005).

Thanks to debates like the one over RU486, we can now see how vital it is that there are more women in our parliaments and in positions of power in general. There is little incentive for many men in parliament to do much more than mouth platitudes about childcare, maternity leave and reproductive rights. However well meaning male power brokers may be (and some of them are very well meaning indeed) these issues mostly remain theoretical or are seen as 'soft' (and therefore unimportant) by a substantial proportion of them. On the contrary, these issues are fundamentally important because the way parents raise the next generation literally creates the future.

These battles are not just about whether women choose to have children or not but also about how they'll parent them. Even as women are finally able to break away from being ruled by their reproductive cycle they are finding that the battle to change social standards around who looks after the kids is daunting and that many segments of society remain resistant to change.

Two steps forward

So, after the excitement, frustrations and turmoil of the last 30 years, where are women now? Well, in some ways we've come a long way and in some ways we haven't. We still have some big battles to fight, and more major changes to make. One thing is certain, however: our naive expectations that the logic of the feminist argument and the justice of the feminist cause would see all barriers fall before it have been well and truly disappointed. While the arguments supporting the agenda have largely been accepted, the action needed to create change simply hasn't eventuated. The disparity between opportunities for men and opportunities for women stubbornly remains – no matter, it seems, how outwardly successful a woman may appear. Here's how a group of ridiculously successful Hollywood female filmmakers discussed it recently:

Lynda Obst: A bunch of us have had this conversation many times over the past couple of decades. What's different for young women filmmakers like Kim and Patty than it was when Nora and Laura and Callie and I were first breaking on the scene, say, in the '80s?

Laura Ziskin: Well, there are four more women directors than there were 20 years ago.

Nora Ephron: No, no, no, no. Twenty years ago there were no women directors. Zero. I was a screenwriter then, and I remember the list that my agent used to give us whenever we finished a script, and there were no women's names on it, none. Maybe, maybe Barbra Streisand –

Ziskin: Now there are four.

Ephron: There aren't four. There are way more than that.

Callie Khouri: But I get lists when I turn in movies, and they don't have a lot of women on them.

Ephron: We've now gotten to a point where we're at the bad plateau, but it's still way more women. It just is. So that is a difference.

Khouri: And yet, still, the good news is that whenever the annual meeting at the Directors Guild takes place, there's never a line for the women's bathroom. ('Chicks Behind Flicks', Rebecca Traister, <Salon.com> 11 October 2007)

When the going gets tough

Attitudes may have changed in some places, but behaviour often hasn't. Progress has been made, but it has been painfully slow. Here we are today — so much already on offer and yet so many obvious indicators of progress stalled. Commentators such as Anne Summers worry the lack of momentum (outlined in her book *The End of Equality*) could be terminal. Progress on such a profound set of social changes is not inexorable, according to academic Leslie Cannold. At a seminar on work and caring in Sydney in 2005 Cannold warned that the danger in current circumstances was that progress for women could not just slow but evaporate. There's no guarantee that the changes made to women's rights will continue — and they could go backwards, she said (National Diversity Think Tank: *Work and Caring Roundtable*, Sydney, 24 October 2005).

At the workplace and at home, in the community and society, at church or in the mosque — and even in the bedroom — women's rights are frequently running into blockages or cul-de-sacs. Yet despite this the topic appears to have literally fallen off the agenda. In the 2007 Australian election campaign there was one word that was notable for its absence: 'women'.

However, before you run off and slit your wrists or murder your boss, the silence about women in the 2007 Federal Election was nevertheless followed by more women entering positions of power than ever before. It was a woman candidate – and outspoken feminist – Maxine McKew who unseated Prime Minister Howard. And it is a woman and feminist – Hillary Clinton – who is at the time of writing one of the most likely Democrat candidates in the 2008 US presidential race. Change is occurring but it simply hasn't been as effortless or as rapid as we hoped it might be. That's because of the enormity of the task, and because it isn't just the workplace that needs to change, or politics or the home. It's all of these and more. Where many women have been extremely successful, however, is in supporting one another. We're living proof of that.

4

In the company of women

We met through another woman who lived around the corner from us and had children at the same primary school as ours. She spotted us as kindred spirits well before we had even connected (thanks, Cindy). Our bond was forged over a regular Friday coffee after walking the kids to school and quickly moved on to much more. Both of us were surprised, given our stage of life and a pretty full address book of friends and colleagues, to find a new partner in crime living virtually next door. Very quickly, but quite naturally, we became close mates. Now we know each other's extended families, we socialise and share weekends away and as our interests have coalesced we have invited each other to professional functions. It feels like we have known each other forever.

We don't agree on everything – not by a long shot. But clearly our fundamental beliefs are similar and there's one in particular that had a bearing on the way we approached this book. It should be imprinted in women's brains: no one is coming to rescue you.

Your prince will never come; your ship will never come in; there are no knights in shining armour. The men of the world are never going to wake up one morning, slap themselves on their collective foreheads and declare; 'Oh, my God, we've been so unfair. Quick, let's share half of everything we've got with women: the power, the money, the status, the decision making. Go for it girls.' If women are going to improve their lot, they're going to have to do it for themselves and for one another.

We've been informally testing this theory for some time now. If there's one tangible result of our friendship it's the 'light bulb' moments when we reframe a problem or frustration for each other or jointly. Sometimes another way of looking at the world or a lesson learned through hard-won experience and then shared makes a big difference. It helps us to find a way to navigate through to the other end despite doubts and confusion. This, along with an invaluable level of emotional support, has been a hallmark of our friendship. It has sustained us in many ways, and has been anchored by our belief in the feminist principles we still swear by which are all about respecting the rights of others.

The importance of wise counsel

Mind you, we were both predisposed to seek solace from wise women, and we've also been lucky enough to have some terrific male friends. Looking back, we've both been able to work with some wonderful mentors at different times in our lives. They were usually older, smarter and more experienced people who encouraged us by identifying something in us we simply hadn't seen ourselves. In those days, mentoring was an informal relationship and motivated by generosity and goodwill. You didn't pay for a mentor back then, and there was no obligation on either side.

Not any more. In fact Jane now gets paid to mentor younger players in business and thoroughly enjoys it. It's a booming business. Young, ambitious employees often mention mentors as essential ingredients for climbing the ladder. Every year the magazine Catherine works for, *AFR Boss*, runs a competition to find a group of outstanding young executives. Invariably as she interviews the six winners, the topic of mentoring comes up again and again. Without mentors, these young people say, they would never have been able to achieve so much. While no one could say this is a bad thing, it's still worth asking what this reveals about our current business structures and relationships in the workplace. What are managers doing, if they are not nurturing and growing their younger members of staff? Well, we all know the answer to that. Business is now so demanding, managers are running hard just to take care of the basics, so they are happy to outsource the human management part of their job. After all, it's often the most complicated.

Nor is it new to pay for emotional support, although the context and language has changed. In her twenties, Jane became depressed and anxious. Struggling to cope, she went into counselling, an experience she found profoundly supportive and life changing. Part of its effectiveness she now believes was that she paid for her therapist to listen to her and so felt entitled to take up all that time simply talking about herself. Counselling was fashionable in the 1970s, now mentoring, life coaching, business coaching – call it what you will – operates in very much the same way.

As workplace dynamics have well and truly changed, job

tenure has shortened and the notion of corporate loyalty has all but disappeared. However, the need for advice and help that extends beyond a yearly performance review remains. We have lost count of the number of young women who ask us for advice on major decisions they have to make about their lives. Sometimes the level of neediness these questions reflect is startling to us. We would have assumed they could ask colleagues or friends and relatives to act as sounding boards. But they are responding to a lack of role models in their workplaces and in their social circles, and they often feel isolated and conflicted. The sheer volume of newspaper articles, seminars, networking events and, yes, books are testament to the hunger women in particular have for a blue print to help them live.

The illusion of having it all

The hunt for a magic cure-all for women facing an array of challenges is as elusive as an effective diet. As commentators on these topics we are often called on to address audiences of slightly anguished women and observing the desperation at close quarters can be a surreal and depressing experience. In a crowded room in a mid-city law firm a young woman approached Catherine soon after a seminar. Clearly distressed, the young woman wanted to know whether she should have children or not, and explained her family were pressuring her about the issue. Culturally, she explained, it was expected young women from her background would study hard, earn a qualification and get a good job but by the time they reached 30 they were also expected to be raising children and retiring from the world of paid work to look after them.

Catherine could only respond by giving her opinion: that talking the issue through more thoroughly with her partner and friends would make sense; looking at how other women blend family and work might help; and most people who end up having children don't regret the decision (apart from the teen years when we all wonder why we ever did it).

A few months later Catherine was interviewing academic and author Professor Barbara Pocock, director of the Centre for Work + Life at the University of South Australia. With Pocock's wealth of experience as an academic and researcher about work and family, Catherine was slightly surprised at her response when asked how she deals with these questions. 'Women are always asking me what to do,' Pocock said. 'Things like "should I have my child now or next year?" I say "work it out, baby." Don't think I've got it figured. No one has.'

Refreshingly, Barbara talked about rejecting the stereotypes and public image of working superwomen and becoming more realistic about what can be done. Take a second look at those constantly held up as iconic achievers, advised Pocock. Westpac CEO Gail Kelly is often portrayed as a woman who 'has it all'. So why hasn't anyone else? asked Pocock. She recalled participating in a radio discussion with the Anglican Archbishop of Sydney, Peter Jensen, and Heather Ridout, the Chief Executive of the employer's peak body, the Australian Industry Group, to discuss the impact of long hours of work on families and Australian society (Friday Panel on Radio National breakfast program, 14 October 2005).

Pocock remembered that Jensen at one stage in the interview remarked that Ridout, who has three children and a clearly demanding job, must have it all together. 'I haven't got it together,' Ridout immediately replied. A high-powered, single, female advertising executive once told Jane something similar. 'You've got a balanced life, after all,' the executive said, 'Well, you know what a balanced life means, don't you?' replied Jane, 'You don't get all of anything.' None of us have got it all worked out – not even the blokes. Life simply isn't like that: no sooner do you cope with one problem than a whole new set reveals itself.

'I talk to a lot of senior women and in public life and very few will say in private life they have got it all together,' Pocock said. 'They say how hard it is holding it together.'

Whose problem is it?

As we've already pointed out in Chapter 1, faced with these demands, many women don't look outwards: they turn inwards. And even with the sheer impact women can have these days as employees, voters and parents, there are plenty of competent and otherwise self-assured women who continue to feel they are on their own in figuring out how to deal with the demands of their life. We know this from our own experience and that of our peers. It's psychologically debilitating for women to feel they 'failed' as mothers, or to ask for help and make demands. Women are often ill equipped to do this because they are supposed to be innately capable of coping and caring in the private domain, just as men are deemed innately equipped to deal with the public sphere.

Certainly when we've been asked for our advice on blending paid work and family life we have tried to give honest responses. The problems encountered, as we've said before, are similar for most women. The arrangements that suit each woman are not identical but often patched together to suit circumstances and stage of life. But we also know how hard it is at times to absorb properly the best advice when you most need it. Exhausted and neurotic with small babies to look after, we have both realised retrospectively that some terrific advice fell on deaf ears. There've been times we haven't listened, haven't trusted our instincts or dared to take a risk – or just haven't recognised the value of input until well after it was offered.

After struggling to keep three young children in after-school care so she could work three days a week, Catherine finally took a friend's advice. She hired a carer to pick the girls up from school and take them home to bathe and feed them instead of doing all that by herself after a long day in the office. It wasn't even much more expensive, as the fees for three children at after school care added up to about the cost of the carer. But Catherine realised she hadn't been thinking the problem through because she was so exhausted and stressed, and had believed in the value of group care. Ironically of course the new arrangement alleviated some of this tension and she wondered why she hadn't done it earlier.

Not all women make the same decisions and changes to their lives at exactly the same time but it's a fair bet many in a peer group have tackled similar challenges. Our experience made us realise a kindred spirit is a major support. We are part of a generation that is pioneering the combination of raising children with paid work and careers so it seems even more important to have some support and advice when forging new territory. Particularly as the new approach contemporary women are taking to parenting makes them so vulnerable to criticism and blame. Mothers today are caught in a bind. Many no longer believe the old, rigid ways of raising children are the best but they don't yet know if the new approach will be any better. As always with raising children, only time will tell.

To help us withstand the temptation to succumb to guilt, insecurity and self-blame, we have instituted our own consciousness-raising and confidence-boosting sessions. Our friendship has been an invaluable source of inspiration and advice. People often bracket friends and family together and while we would never underestimate the importance of family for women with children, family also represents work. You can choose your friends but not your family, the saying goes, and familial intimacy can obscure rather than shed light on how to get through tough times. And once you have your own children, wherever they go, the chores follow. The old joke about a family holiday being an oxymoron is funny because it's true.

Female friendships

Good friendship on the other hand, is pure support — hence the stampede by women into book clubs or women's networks in the workplace and new mothers into mothers' groups. Unlike the hierarchical nature of mentoring, these forums are about sharing experience between peers as much as analysing books, work and kids. Jane remembers the night her book club was discussing Helen Garner's thoughtful exploration of sexual harassment *The First Stone*. As the discussion unfolded it became clear that almost every woman there had experienced unwanted sexual attention from an authority figure when young. Most of the sexual touching was fairly mild, but not all of it. The mere act of discussing their own experiences with one another, triggered by reading this book, had a therapeutic effect. At the very least, their shared feelings of shame and shock were normalised. The women discovered they were not alone in having attracted such unpleasant and unwanted attention, and that their emotional responses – their shame and guilt – was not unique to them either.

This is another gift to women of our generation from feminism. Once, women kept such experiences buried deep within themselves, convinced they alone had brought on such attentions, deeply ashamed about what people might think if such incidents were ever revealed. Now women have discovered such experiences are common and most importantly of all not our fault. If as some psychologists have claimed you are only as psychically sick as your biggest secret, then a whole generation of women just got a lot better. The remarkable and brave refusal of Sydney rape victim Tegan Wagner to allow her name to be withheld because she felt it implied she had something to be ashamed of is yet another example of the powerful way our new-found openness and truth telling has helped many wounded women to heal. This is profoundly important stuff, and Wagner's brave stand won her the prestigious Edna Ryan Award from the Women's Electoral Lobby in 2006.

While we fortunately did not have to deal with the level of abuse and distress that some women do, it took the two of us many years of struggling with the competing priorities of caring, family, community and the formal workplace to help each other to understand we were not always the problem. To stop feeling our employers were doing us a favour by tolerating our part-time hours. To realise we were doing our best with our kids, and that didn't mean we were always right or fair. To learn that what we were encountering was part of a much bigger conflict around social change and the right to lead a full life. Colleagues, friends, partners and a few very wise people we have met along the way have all helped us see a clearer picture about the complexity of women's lives. They have helped us understand we are part of social and economic structures, bearing the weight of many expectations.

Conventional friendship

The strength of a good friend, the kind who leaves you feeling better for seeing them, is that they are often the only people who can remind you that you have the right to your own space and point of view. That not everything you do – particularly once you have turned yourself into that cultural icon called a mother – has to be for the benefit of someone else. It is an act of friendship to draw you away from the role of martyr and doormat. Surprisingly, we have not had to do very much of that for one another, but we have helped each other to stop beating ourselves up.

And we believe it is also an act of friendship to avoid the my-house-is-better-than-yours, my-kid-is-smarter-than-yours, point-scoring kind of female relationship as well. Most women have a gift for close friendship. Contrary to the old fashioned, male-generated myth that all women are in bitter competition with one another to catch the prize (a man), female friendships, at their best, have been supporting and nurturing women for centuries. Feminism developed out of these networks, such as the old consciousness-raising groups from women's liberation days – female friendships by another name. And perhaps because they so commonly happen under the radar our friendships are often subversive. They certainly have been in our case.

There is of course the corollary to that: the kind of female friendships that often police women's behaviour by making sure no one steps outside the boundaries of 'acceptable' standards. Much of the famous bitchiness between teenage girls is about this kind of disapproval and mutual moral guardianship, as is the supposed war between paid and non-paid working mothers (see Chapter 9). It is our observation that this kind of purse-lipped relationship between women is on the decline and beginning to look very old-fashioned. Another unforeseen benefit of feminism perhaps is the potential to end such self-defeating behaviour.

Nevertheless, it must be acknowledged that this kind of moralising between women is probably a legacy of the first wave of feminism. This was the era around the end of the 19th and beginning of the 20th centuries, when women across the developed world – including Australia – sought the right to vote. As part of their campaign, the more conservative suffragists and highly influential women's temperance societies sought to justify women's rights. They emphasised women's 'superior' moral character over – in particular – working-class and drunken men. A useful strategy at the time, its legacy can still be seen in the usually mistaken view that modern or 'second-wave' feminism remains puritanical, humourless and disapproving. And it may have something to do with the enduring female stereotypes (see Chapter 10) which are often used to rationalise informal discrimination against women.

By allowing women to have broader life experiences, feminism has helped take the intensity out of our informal relationships. We'd argue that female friendships are more robust now precisely because we are not all being forced to compete around the same narrow domestic agenda. Put simply, we have other things to talk about.

Subversive friendship

Australian feminist Anne Summers' famous book title *Damned Whores and God's Police* illustrated the way women were restricted by polarised social roles. There has been a slow shift as women begin to inhabit a wider range of options across cultural and economic arenas. In the process, as we have pointed out, some of the moralistic pressure of the traditional divisions has relaxed. As a result women's relationships with one another have also changed, becoming less critical, more confident and a lot more fun. The remarkable ITV dramatisation of the experiences of a real wartime British housewife – 'Housewife 49' – illustrated the gradual blossoming that can take place when women leave the isolation of their households and come together in work and, eventually, friendship with other women. There have been such moments of community and freedom outside the domestic domain for women over the years, but until now, they have been the exception rather than the norm. It is often when women are gathered together, usually over a couple of glasses of wine or a coffee – that their humour finds its most anarchic expression.

Mothers, despite their often peachy-keen portrayal in the media, have usually developed a mordantly funny view of the world and our place in it. Our husbands, children, neighbours, colleagues, bosses, parents and in-laws would find some of our conversations surprising. Just like the boys do in bars after work, women unload to one another and so recharge their batteries. A friend loves to tell the story about the suburban street in Sydney where every Friday evening returning husbands and children had to go from house to house to find where their wives or mothers had settled for their weekly alcohol-fuelled debrief. It was pizza all round every Friday and damn the childhood obesity.

Interestingly, this behaviour in men is called bonding, and regarded with a certain amount of indulgence and good humour. In women it is still usually considered if not quite bitching then certainly irresponsible. Let's face it, women gathered together sometimes make men uneasy. When Catherine and another woman worked as court reporters they were dubbed the Madame Defarges of the commercial division; and Catherine was also called a witch twice in one day at work because she was spotted talking to another woman of a certain age. An exchange student who lived with Jane's family in the 1970s once angrily called the women of the household 'hens' because they had been laughing and talking around the kitchen table for an hour or two. Yet how many prescriptions for tranquilisers and anti-depressants has such conviviality among women prevented? We all need to vent sometimes, and mothers and carers need to do so more than most.

Nurturing friendships between women can often be the most empowering relationships in our lives. When our kids go through a rough patch, when our marriages collapse, when our parents become old and ill and demanding, it is usually our female friends we turn to for support. They listen to us and empathise, but they do more than that. They bring round casseroles and mind children, they feed pets and collect newspapers, they attend funerals and pour us glasses of wine and coax us to forget the diet. They also take the pressure off our husbands, by giving us the emotional and therapeutic support many men are unwilling or find hard to provide. And in return they ask nothing more from us than what they have already given. And such is the nature of a female friend; it is often a woman's friendship that a man will rely on when his marriage collapses because when he loses his wife, he often loses his closest emotional support. Maybe that's one of the reasons why most marriage breakups are instigated by women (see Chapter 9); they know their friends will support them even if their husband will not.

Well before our friendship was forged, a blend of family and role models from different parts of our lives along with a whole raft of experiences provided many lessons. Our parents of course were our compasses as we grew up. And our mothers in particular showed us the importance of grasping the opportunities they had been denied. Catherine's mother Patricia urged her girls to aim high and travel the world. Although she had left school at 15, as was common at the time, Patricia had travelled to London where she lived and worked for two years before returning to Sydney, marrying and 'settling down'. In fact, Patricia never did settle down and her feisty behaviour and outward focus was very different from many of her contemporaries and a source of great embarrassment to her daughter, until Catherine realised just how lucky she was. Patricia's exhortations to avoid rushing into marriage also were heeded – her daughters didn't exactly stampede up the aisle.

Jane's mother shared many of Patricia's characteristics. She also expected as much of her daughters as from her son and was also feisty and outwardly focused. Her journey from the conventional – secretarial college, office job, marriage and stay-at-home motherhood – to university-educated, proudly feminist relationships counsellor was both remarkable and inspirational. She also exhorted her daughters not to rush into marriage and babies, frankly counselling them not to do as she had done. She may have felt she had taught her daughters rather too well when she reached her sixties without any sign of a grandchild. Twenty years on, she has six of them, all girls. 'We're maintaining the quality' she often says.

Loving our weaknesses

Strong friendship between women knows few boundaries. The intense relationship women have with how they look and their bodies can often be expressed only to a female friend. There are many reasons for this preoccupation. No doubt partly because of the increase in visual technology in our society the pressure on women to conform to certain standards of beauty has magnified. Factors such as the mass production of clothing has also increased women's insecurity about their size and shape. Once, when women either made their own clothes or had them made by a professional dressmaker, they simply took their own measurements and the garment was tailored accordingly. Now women must conform to standard sizes and shopping – although many seem to be addicted to it – has become, at least for those of us with a less than perfect shape, traumatic.

Few modern women of any age feel entirely comfortable inside their own skins, and almost all of us would like to lose at least five kilos. It's a paradox that this preoccupation has reached such proportions just as women are no longer obliged to depend on gaining a husband for financial and physical protection. Or is it because of the speed of this revolution that women cling to old-fashioned ideas about appearance? Men, it should be noted, are also subject to the pressure to look good but it doesn't seem to reach such extremes. Their goal appears to be more about looking fit and powerful, with the secondary reason to attract a partner. Many women turning to surgery and chemicals are aiming to look sexy, for men, presumably.

To their credit, many men find this obsession with appearance unfathomable. They fancy us, whether we're size 8 or 16. But those who sneer at this appearance fetish would do well to remember how much more pressure is brought to bear on women to look attractive and slim. Or even, as we will examine in Chapter 11, to replicate porn star chic with surgically enhanced boobs, bleached hair and the ability to pole dance. This extreme emphasis on appearance doesn't just apply to young women either, with the demand for botox injections and facelifts in the suburbs indicating women of all ages are reacting to higher and higher standards and the need to look perfect. Urged to look sexy and alluring by mass media and peers, women then tend to be blamed for breaking the unspoken rules if they don't look prim and proper in a shop, office or factory.

There are rules for men as well. In fact, men have even fewer choices about what they can wear to work, but there are advantages. The rules are clearer and easier for them to follow, as long as they conform and are neat and tidy. Granted there is less latitude for diversion from a suit or pair of overalls, but men also face less judgment based on appearance. Given all of this, worrying about and sustaining each other on the vexed issue of how we look is far from a silly little diversion. It is an understandable reaction to the pressure for women to look good at all costs and explains why many feel constantly unhappy or somehow unworthy if they don't make an effort or look as attractive as they are told they should. Body image issues preoccupied us for many years no matter how hard we tried to convince ourselves of the futility of agonising over that extra inch on our hips or the rolls on our stomachs. How we wish we could have back all the time we spent in this useless psychological torture.

Often enough the only respite was with our friends, when we could most satisfyingly share our mutual insecurity. 'Does my bum look big in this?' as only a female friend can understand, is really a request for reassurance. Tell me I look OK, women are begging, that I am not freakish, that I do not really look the way I fear I do. Many women it seems have lost the ability to actually see themselves and we narrow our eyes as we approach a mirror to deliberately lose focus and avoid undermining our confidence. We are not alone is this subterfuge. Now in her mid-sixties, film writer and author Nora Ephron in *I Feel Bad About My Neck* pinpoints another technique:

> I try as much as possible not to look in the mirror. If
> I pass a mirror, I avert my eyes. If I must look into it,
> I begin by squinting, so that if anything really bad is
> looking back at me, I am already halfway to closing

my eyes to ward off the sight. And if the light is good (which I hope it's not) I often do what so many women my age do when stuck in front of a mirror: I gently pull the skin of my neck back and stare wistfully at a younger version of myself. (Ephron 2006, p.16)

Sanity saving

In private, many women strike poses and then dress to cover their flaws. They ricochet between a desire to accept themselves as they are and an equally irresistible desire to become their ideal, disciplined, sculpted, skinny, best self. Some of us start a diet every morning and break it every afternoon. Understandably this drives our husbands or partners and children bonkers, but our female friends totally understand it. After all, they do much the same themselves, and true friendship isn't actually about helping us to improve or become more sensible − that is perhaps the role of a more formally therapeutic relationship. Real friendship is about giving one another the space to be exactly who we are − with ridiculous insecurities, self-defeating behaviours and all. Yes, we want our friends to lie and say we look thinner, but we also want them to ask us the same questions, so we can kindly lie to them as well. Many women have discovered friends like each other for their weaknesses, and it's their strengths that are often much harder to bear.

And that's why our ability not just to share our sense of insecurity about our looks with one another but the continuous tricks our bodies seem determined to play on us remain so important. It is with other women that we can confide our concerns about regular and irregular periods, about fearing being pregnant or not being pregnant. It is with other women – particularly new mothers – that we can share our birth stories, over and over, and over again if necessary, as we try to integrate this earth-shattering experience into our psyche. We can talk of stitches and torn perinea and salt-water baths and blood and shit and vernix. Of mastitis and cracked nipples and hilarious accidents with baby poo and vomit and pee. We can also talk of orgasms and contraception and abortions and sperm and vaginal secretions and g-spots and lack of desire and infections. And later of hot flushes and flooding and dry vaginas and sagging tits and flaccid bellies and incipient moustaches and all the aches that our flesh is prone to.

Once women are really friends, there is no subject that remains taboo. Female friendships at their most intimate may come the closest to being able to share fully with another human being just exactly what it feels like to be you. They make life a little easier for women when they are far too concerned with keeping up appearances. And on a much broader level this female solidarity, as we shall see, has also played a fundamental role in establishing an agenda around women's rights. It was at the very heart of early feminist activism. It's not so fashionable to talk in such terms today but collective pressure may be the only way to change the stubborn norms of household work, which we now examine.

5

Hard labour

'To make a mess that another person will have to deal with – the dropped socks, the toothpaste sprayed on the bathroom mirror, the dirty dishes left from a late-night snack – is to exert domination in one of its more silent and intimate forms.' – Barbara Ehrenreich

It's early evening and almost dark walking back from the railway station to home after the daily commute. The houses we walk past are lit up and in some a kitchen can be glimpsed with a woman toiling over a bench or bending over a child as they finish their homework. We should be there, we find ourselves thinking guiltily, cooking dinner and chatting to the kids about their day, propping up the family and performing the ritual tasks of the household. Getting a decent, home-cooked meal ready for the tribe.

As mothers who also work outside the home we are both

familiar with this feeling, this surge of emotion and regret around not being in the 'right' place in that crucial early-evening period. It isn't just the cooking or chatting or any other element of the scenario that has made us feel remiss. It is the sense we have failed in some fundamental way and let down the entire family. It's a feeling and a role that is difficult to shake off.

It is intensely disappointing to us that we still need to include a chapter on housework in a book about women's lives. If this book was about the men who were born at the same time as we were, it is inconceivable that there would be such a chapter. This speaks volumes about how much of a dead weight home and family can still be to women. Nevertheless, it must be discussed if women are ever going to free themselves from the yoke of doing most of the housework.

A woman's place

The burden women bear as the lynchpin of the domestic environment is much more than a list of 'to do' items – it is a role so heavily imbued with emotion, guilt and judgement that it's a minefield even to discuss. Men tend to get stroppy or poke fun at the whole subject while women become defensive, angry or just weary at going over the same old ground. Women are still considered 'naturally' better at home chores than men and more attuned to the needs of the household. As mothers and wives, we have done our fair share of carping about incompetent men in our time too, but it's also apparent to us that learned helplessness is at play and with a bit of practice and attention any man can actually apply the same skills they use in their jobs to run a household.

There are exceptions to this, of course. A married man of our acquaintance in a management position is unusual in his acceptance of the dual responsibility of caring for kids and the home. However, he was sent to all-male boarding schools at six, his mother died when he was young and his father primarily identified as gay. This man never saw a woman running around picking up after him or any other man, so he grew up not to expect it either. What does this say about the kind of example women in traditional families set for their sons and their daughters?

Forget the fact that these household tasks are so basic that anyone can do them because that's not the point. Tethering women psychologically to this workload allows female stereotypes to be propped up and ultimately helps undermine any lasting or widespread change in women's status. It keeps us with our arms immersed in suds at the kitchen sink or changing the nappies while the 'real work', we are told, goes on elsewhere.

Over years of reflection on the disparity of this social order, it is increasingly apparent to us that even reallocating housework is not enough – it is time to desanctify it as well. There is nothing edifying or inherently uplifting about most chores, no matter what the latest book or opinion article tells you. It is, in the words of outspoken American author Linda Hirshman ('Firing another volley in the "Mommy Wars"', Suzy Hansen, *LA Times*, 27 June, 2006) 'repetitious, it's done in private, it's boring.' It's rubbish to say we should honour housework more, she says, and that it's just because women do it that we don't value it. 'The reason we don't value it is because it's not very highly skilled in a society that values education above all things.'

It's also struck us that those justifying the status quo around domestic work are usually the ones who don't do much of it. Catherine recalls the parish priest in his weekly sermon often describing in glowing terms the role of housewife and the uplifting nature of caring for a family, making beds, cooking and dusting, before he finished Mass, walked out of the church and sat down to his Sunday lunch served by his housekeeper. It was explained to a young Catherine that he couldn't get married and so, as a man, he had to have a housekeeper to cook and clean for him. A female housekeeper, as it happened. It reminds us of that old saying: I love work; I could watch it all day.

'A woman's place is in the home' is not a statement of fact, even though we've both been told that this is the natural order and 'just the way things are'. The role of housewife has its roots in the early stages of industrialisation in the late 18th century when jobs became increasingly based in offices and factories. Home work was for women and real paid work was for men and this division of labour was reinforced by the belief that men belonged in the work place because they were naturally more competitive and aggressive, while women belonged at home because they were naturally more suited to nurturing and raising children. This hierachy of roles extended into the class system.

Domesticity was 'invented as a strategy to differentiate the middle class from the working class. For well over two centuries having a wife at home has signalled middle-class status' Joan Williams tells us (Williams 2000, p. 157). It still does.

A recent survey found that fully two-thirds of Americans believe it would be best for women to stay home and care for family and children. Domesticity's descriptions of

men and women persist in vernacular gender talk such as
John Gray's *Men are from Mars, Woman are from Venus*,
as well as in the strain of feminist theory that associates
women with an ethic of care. (Williams 2000, p.2)

This allocation of a certain aptitude for loving and caring to the female gender sets up another damaging double standard, where women who venture into the public sphere then have to live up to much higher expectations of behaviour, ethics and altruism, as we will examine further in Chapter 6.

It seems to us that challenging the status quo on housework has gone the same way as talking about feminism. It is seen as political correctness gone mad, or radical, left-wing ratbaggery. Women we know mutter about the unfairness but swiftly justify the division of labour at home with the fact their husband is the main income earner or just takes too long to get things done, despite clearly being possessed of reasonable intelligence and health. Learned helplessness is a widespread phenomenon in the face of domestic chores.

Women absorb the message about their responsibility at home from the time they can understand by watching their own mothers. Their strongest early role models are about women and care and what that means in the home. Poor mothering and household maintenance is a crime, if popular depictions are to be believed, and destroys the very social fabric we cherish. Yet if poor housekeeping was a mark of failure we would be outcasts from society. We hate housework, are not very good at it and will take help whenever possible. If we could quit this particular job we would. Today.

Good housekeeping

If women are to have a chance of a full and satisfying life then there has to be a shift around the way the domestic workload and caring is allocated, physically and emotionally. It is an equity issue, but it also has to do with the quality of women's lives and their control over their destiny. Much housework is not just drudgery, it is also usually unpaid and thankless too, unless you are male – when it is quite likely to win you praise no matter how small or badly completed the job. Of course, we should add here that much market work is similarly boring and mundane (and is often performed by women), but at least the results are more tangible and you get paid.

Just because domestic labour is completed in the home shouldn't mean it's viewed as less legitimate work. Women who take on these roles are working and it's insulting to say otherwise. As Joan Williams points out, a woman who stays at home to care for children does a lot more than that. She irons shirts, prepares meals and maintains the house which benefits everyone who lives there. No wonder when a woman stays at home full or even part of the time, the amount of domestic work her husband does falls dramatically. Don't we know it. Statistics show that although the breakdown of home chores isn't particularly equitable anywhere in the world, women in Australia still tend to do quite a lot of housework compared to other countries. Australian academic Michael Bittman has been studying time use, gender and impact on families for three decades and hasn't seen much change in who does what around the house over that period ('Enjoying yourself Mum, or just out of breath?' Trish Bolton, *The Age*, 13 December 2004).

Women in Australia do around 77 per cent of unpaid work, compared to 70 per cent in Sweden and 88 per cent in Italy ('The Rush Hour', Michael Bittman and Judy Wajcman, Social Policy Research Centre discussion paper, February 1999). Unpaid work continues to be largely women's work and this has social costs for women in both earnings and the quality of their leisure according to Bittman's studies. In fact, women's leisure time is lower quality than men's, according to a study, because it is usually interrupted and fitted in between chores.

There's also plenty of international data showing women's share of housework remains onerous no matter what their personal or work circumstances may be. We were struck by the study 'Time Allocation within the Family' (*Economic Journal*, Helene Couprie, 2007) which looked at working women, single or living with a partner, both with and without children. It found single working women spent an average of ten hours a week doing housework and single men seven hours. After becoming a couple, women's housework time shot up to 15 hours a week, while the average male contribution dropped to five hours, even when both spouses work outside the home. Indeed, Jane used to 'joke' that when she and Ralph lived together, but had no children, the housework was divided 50/50. After the first child it became 70/30, and with the second it dropped to 90/10. She decided not to have any more children.

Meanwhile expectations around the investment required for housework and parenting just keep on intensifying. What passed for a nice home (as Kath and Kim would say) a few years ago would not pass muster in these days of makeover and renovation TV show mania, and the middle-class preoccupation with property. In the realm of household chores, there's been a move to shift the goal posts for what constitutes a clean home. We have been astonished by the fascination the Australian public has for cleaning tips as reflected in the best-selling books *Spotless* and *Speed Cleaning* (oddly enough, we haven't rushed out to buy them). Authors Shannon Lush and Jennifer Fleming are certainly on to something with their household guides in which they answer those tricky cleaning questions. They argue their readers are interested in smarter and quicker ways to clean with less time available and they certainly recommend less use of expensive chemical cleaners.

But this fascination with cleaning also reflects the ever-escalating standards for such chores, in much the same way the modern requirements for 'good parenting' grow more and more demanding and complicated. In fact, there is a lengthy list of examples of how expectations of the standards we keep at home continue to rise exponentially. No longer can you shove meat and three veg in front of your husband and kids. No, thanks to Nigella, Jamie, Gordon, Stephanie et al, with their TV shows and best-selling cookbooks, it must be healthy, balanced and cordon bleu. And God forgive the mother who admits to serving take-away!

This sounds suspiciously like another part of the backlash against women who are venturing too far too fast and getting too uppity by half. In the same era in which women's participation in the paid labour force has increased, there has been growing emphasis on domestic and caring work becoming more elaborate, more time-consuming and more 'feminine' than ever. This kind of alignment only exists in the domestic sphere of course, where cooking a nightly meal is mainly unsung women's work. Funnily, our top professional chefs are still mostly men.

Such distinctions also reinforce the notion that domestic

labour is not worthy of praise, and help perpetuate its low value in our society. The tragedy of housework is that when it is done really well, it is invisible. You only notice housework when it isn't done. The much ridiculed 'Don't walk on my nice clean floor' is actually the cry of a frustrated and infuriated worker who resents that her hard labour goes unseen and is unending.

Mother dearest

The same dynamic operates with standards for childcare that have become absurdly time-consuming. Kids not given a full range of stimulating activities and adult focus from the time of conception are now deemed to be at risk of delinquency (see Chapter 8). Yet even our mothers, rearing four children each in the 1950s and '60s, rarely spent one-on-one time with us. They couldn't – they were too busy. It was considered unnecessary or even damaging to pay children too much individual attention because you could risk raising spoilt brats. The hothouse and helicopter parenting norms of the 21st century leave our mothers laughing in disbelief.

It's also been intriguing to track the discussion on the merits and pitfalls of having children cared for outside the home. Some thoughtful work has been conducted into the effects of too many hours of formal day care on the under twos, particularly in Anne Manne's book *Motherhood – how should we care for our children?*, where she argues for more recognition of the role of mothers and a need to provide many more options to accommodate the combination of mothering with other caring responsibilities, paid work or study.

There has been a much more hysterical beat up (particularly

in the media) on the apparently appalling and permanent ill effects of childcare centres and long day care on children's development just as women need to rely more and more on such services. Evidence to the contrary seems to be given far less oxygen, despite a growing body of research showing most kids benefit from some preschool care. According to Michael Keane, Professor of Economics at University of Technology Sydney, there is no evidence of any adverse effects on kids in well-run and well-resourced formal childcare.

> Quality day care and pre schooling could help raise the intelligence levels of young children and were of greater benefit to their long-term future than later interventions, such as tuition subsidies for university students. (*Sydney Morning Herald*, 31 August 2007)

Few people, least of all us, would say children don't need their parents around them when they are young. But it's becoming clear a mixture of different environments and people is not a bad thing for most kids. In fact another study in 2006 by Professor Tony Vinson of Sydney University found that children who were not sent to preschool were starting school without knowing how to hold a pen or paintbrush. While that may not have a long-term effect, it's certainly not fair to say kids kept by their mother's side are automatically getting the best start in life. This is particularly so when it is used to make women in paid work feel guilty and remiss. Some critics of childcare have been sweeping in their condemnation particularly of mothers of children under two. However, the issue is multi-layered and complex. It is too easy to say all babies and toddlers will do better at home with Mum. If Mum is happy to have them home full time, this is probably spot-on, but if she is miserable, depressed, poor or lonely the opposite may be true.

Of course, debates about the effects of childcare on young children remain theoretical if parents can't find or afford a suitable option. Formal childcare remains expensive, despite government rebates, and simply unavailable for people in regional areas. The well-intentioned use of accreditation to ensure high standards in childcare centres has imposed higher costs in the sector, which is rapidly becoming dominated by commercial operators such as ABC Learning, set up to make a profit and subject to the vagaries of the financial markets (as the company's plummeting share price in early 2008 showed).

Family day care remains difficult to find and is concentrated in urban areas, while nannies are just too expensive for many parents. Regardless of the care option chosen, the cost usually comes out of post-tax earnings, making much childcare so expensive that a woman has to earn a significant amount to justify having a job at all. Working out how much income you need to make it worthwhile to be in paid employment is a common equation for mothers. At one stage Catherine had about $50 a week left from her salary after childcare was deducted (interestingly, it's nearly always the mother's usually-smaller salary that is expected to take the hit). And it's unsurprising that this is the point when a significant number of mothers leave formal workplaces.

Given all these financial and emotional factors many women around Australia are relying on family and friends to care for their children and then make sacrifices of their own personal time to ensure they have as much contact with their kids as they can. Recent studies are showing that many working mothers actually spend on average as much time with their children as homemakers. This apparent paradox has been examined by UNSW academic Lyn Craig ('How do they do it? A time-diary analysis of how working mothers find time for kids', Social Policy Research Centre Discussion Paper, January 2005) who found that parents maintain their time commitments to both work and childcare by a suite of strategies, including reducing the time devoted to other activities (principally sleep, leisure, bathing, dressing, grooming, eating) and rescheduling activities (from weekends to weekday or changing the time of day at which particular activities are undertaken).

But no matter what strategies they employ, the failure to address the lack of affordable childcare options is sparking plenty of anger from mothers in the community and across socio-economic groups. At a range of forums on the issue, Catherine has heard irate women talk about the sheer unfairness of Australia's response to the crisis. While these are not women who necessarily identify as feminists, their articulation of these concerns and the need for change reflects a strong feminist tradition of identifying and then drawing attention to the plight of women.

Families are also exploiting the love and goodwill of grandparents, asking them to fill the void left by a lack of accessible childcare. Just when many women feel that at last they have the time and space to do what they want, after a lifetime of putting others' needs first, their daughters and sons come cap in hand begging them to take on child-caring duties once more. Many grandparents enjoy this work, and it is good to see (and is a direct result of feminism) so many grandfathers actively caring for small children – making up for their lack of such hands-on contact with their own children, perhaps. Yet we can't help feeling that childcare provided by grandparents should be voluntary, not unavoidable.

Outsourcing

While women largely remain the watchdogs of childcare and home duties, the trend to outsource domestic and caring work has made for an emotional and revealing debate. We have noticed when housework is outsourced to a cleaner, especially in households that contain a woman, the castigation from all parts of the political and social spectrum comes thick and fast. This has been the subject of some serious sociological examination, particularly in the US. There is a fairly widespread tendency by middle-class American families to employ household help and nannies mainly from a pool of low-skilled migrants, thus creating an underclass of domestic help that bears a striking resemblance to the servants in better off homes a few generations ago. In Australia there has been a similar trend, although not on quite the scale of the US, where access to the largely-Latino labour source has had an impact. Remember the Clinton-era Attorney General nominees Zoe Baird and Kimba Wood, both highly-paid professionals who were forced to withdraw after it was discovered they had employed illegal migrants as domestic help or nannies? The cultural phenomenon of the book *The Nanny Diaries* and the subsequent film, where the women who use nannies are portrayed as unnatural monsters of vanity and egoism, are revealing of continuing social disapproval of women who choose to get paid help.

Nevertheless, most of our friends have some sort of cleaning help coming to their homes weekly and have used paid childcare. We have been through guilt about this process and emerged unscathed the other side. Even the best-argued objections to paid domestic support seem underpinned by a traditional notion that women should really bear the responsibility for household work, whether they perform the job or not. Are they abrogating their womanly duty by seeking this help? Would we apply the same scrutiny to a man employing a cleaner? Not if Catherine's parish priest was any guide. If household work has been rendered invisible because women did most of it, then paying a cleaner makes it visible again. But, unfortunately, it doesn't change the gender division of labour.

And what do you know — getting a cleaner sees women being criticised for having unrealistic standards, being martyrs or exploiting poorer women. So when employed women can afford to pay for some help or even buy an occasional take-away meal they are leapt on for being lazy, or worse selfish and irresponsible. They are even, according to the popular media, contributing to childhood obesity and the rise in diabetes by not preparing a homecooked meal. It is intriguing that a single father taking his kids to Maccas is to be congratulated for spending time with them, while a single mother would be castigated. As a woman, you really can't win.

Needless to say, paying for domestic services is not an option for most women. Particularly not for women on low incomes, or single mothers who can ill afford to spend part of their hard-won salary on such luxuries. It's the same financial bind that faces many women looking for childcare.

The link between home and work

In recent years some attention has started to be paid to the vexed issue of gender and unpaid work partly because the link between what goes on inside and outside the home is starting to become more evident. The findings of inequality in the home around the hours of housework (unearthed by researcher Helene Couprie) reflected those in the workplace. 'The quickest way to improve the situation at home would be for women to gain equality at work in terms of pay and opportunities,' Couprie found. As long as women's work is invisible, unrewarded or taken for granted, it will tend to be undervalued everywhere.

In early 2005, then Federal Sex Discrimination Commissioner Pru Goward announced a study of the gender divide in housework and childcare. Statistics show Australian women perform about 90 per cent of childcare as well as the lion's share of household chores. It became a constant theme for Goward during the remainder of her term (she stepped down from the role to enter NSW State Parliament).

> If we are serious about helping people to balance paid work and family obligations then we need to get serious about creating greater equality in the division of caring and household tasks ... (in Adele Horin, *Sydney Morning Herald*, 5 February 2005)

Paid leave for parents is usually only provided as maternity leave, and worse this remains available to very few. And in the rare cases where it is an option, paternity leave is generally not used. The overwhelming evidence from employers with these provisions is that most men don't take it up, possibly because there is a stigma attached. This is not just a perception, as there is a long-term career penalty for taking advantage of such parental provisions. It's just that at the moment it is mostly women who are obliged to pay it. But studies also reveal that men who bond with their babies at this crucial time have a stronger long-term involvement with their children and their care.

We are aware of some couples who have been lucky enough — financially speaking — to be able to swap traditional roles and the father has taken over running the house while the mother pursues a career. But we're wary about reading too much into it because the cases are isolated and largely from privileged backgrounds. It can also be the case that finely laid plans are easily derailed. We interviewed two women who were the main breadwinners in their homes and their partners were not employed but still refused to do any housework. It seems there remains a kind of default to the male breadwinner model even if the traditional earning roles are reversed.

When it comes to workforce patterns and housework the majority of employees on part-time hours are women who then use their 'time off' for domestic and caring chores (but only after the kids' needs have been tended to, according to Lyn Craig's research on women's time use). Women also make up a disproportionate number of casual and contract workers, with low-security and low-paid jobs. For them the penalty of part-time work is very real but, given the cost of childcare, it is the only way they can care for the family and earn an income. They are also unable to upgrade their skills by taking time off to study or train which has a compounding impact on their life-long earning potential and ability to put money away for their old age (more about this in Chapter 7). This reinforces women's role as prime carers and housekeepers and their marginalisation as employees.

Many women say they crave more flexible hours, and it's certainly a formula we are very familiar with having both worked part-time for years. But it's the assumption we would remain disproportionately responsible for running the house that then becomes even harder to alter. After all, if you spend more time at home then isn't it your duty to do even more of the housework? And this assumption locks both genders into inflexible roles.

Many mothers in the paid workforce, meanwhile, are criticised for leaving early in the day, or not carrying their weight at work. While there may be some truth in this at times, particularly when children are sick, it ignores the reality that most are conscientious and only too aware of the difficulty in finding flexible work. Most mothers in the workplace, from our experience, are time sensitive and efficient but unable to stick around to impress the boss. Catherine remembers standing at the lift in her office building at 5.30 pm one afternoon after working hard to meet her deadlines and about to rush over to the childcare centre and then to after school care before getting home to bath, feed and settle three young children. A colleague (who had three children, but also a wife) walked past and said 'Some people are lucky.' Too angry and upset to reply, all she could think of in response was 'Yeah, really, really lucky.'

Sometimes the competing demands of work and family can reach a farcical level. A senior advertising executive of our acquaintance gathered his team around him at 7 pm and announced yet another last-minute panic on a job for a particularly difficult client. 'Drop everything,' he said, 'It's going to be another all-nighter.' A senior woman in the team stood up and told him she could not stay. It was her son's seventh birthday and she hadn't even bought him a present yet. 'Come on, love, get your priorities right,' was her boss's unsympathetic response. She picked up her bag, looking at him hard. 'You are absolutely right,' she said, and left, never to return.

More often women find a way to fulfil all their competing obligations, but at some cost to themselves and, sometimes, to their children. A few years ago, Jane was in the middle of completing the post-production for a million-dollar TV advertising campaign. This required that she attend edits, sound recording and mixing sessions, all booked long in advance and highly expensive, with hundreds of dollars ticking away for every minute in the studio. On her busiest day her youngest daughter woke too ill to attend school. Her husband was away on business, her parents unavailable and no childcare was to be found at such short notice. Jane bundled poor Charlotte up and took her from edit suite to recording studio, from recording studio to post-production house. On each cab ride, Charlotte bravely and uncomplainingly vomited into the bowl Jane had brought for the purpose and Jane washed it out as soon as they arrived at the next appointment. Almost a decade later, Jane still feels guilty at the memory but what else could she do? Given her professional responsibility for her client's money she could not cancel the sessions (cancellation fees for such expensive facilities are exorbitant and on-air deadlines were looming) and given her personal responsibilities she could not leave an ill daughter at home to fend for herself. Unsatisfactory though her solution was for everyone, she did the best she could.

Leaving the woman holding the baby (pun intended) is not just unfair and draining. It has an impact on the entire family. US sociologist Arlie Hochschild's work found 'American families were serving as a shock absorber of a stalled gender revolution. The move of masses of women into the paid workforce has constituted a revolution. But the slower shift in ideas of "manhood", the resistance to sharing work at home, the rigid schedules at work make for a "stall" in this gender revolution ...' (Arlie Hochschild, *The Commercialisation of Intimate Life*, 2003, p. 28)

We're aware that paid work is not a bed of roses for blokes or single women either. Many labour in dull and repetitive jobs, or under lousy bosses who make unreasonable demands. However, while many men lament their long hours at work some will admit when pressed that they don't want to pick up a share of the unrewarded and unapplauded second shift chores either. We've worked with many of them, and occasionally accepted their offer of a drink after 5 pm and delegated the feeding and bedtime shift to our respective husbands. A course of action we'd quietly like to recommend to more women. Far from being irresponsible, it gives you time out and the dads time to bond with their kids. The underlying problem unfortunately is not as easily alleviated.

Emotional labour

Work inside the home is not always about chores. One of the most onerous roles is managing the dynamics of the home. The running of the schedule, the attention to details about band practice and sports training, the purchase of presents for next Saturday's birthday party, the check up at the dentist, all usually fall on one person's shoulders. Woody Allen, in the much-publicised custody case for his children with Mia Farrow, eventually lost, in part because unlike Farrow, he could not name the children's dentist or pediatrician. It's a guardianship role and it is not only physically time consuming but demands enormous intellectual and emotional attention.

Sociologists call it kin work. It involves:

> keeping in touch with relations, preparing holiday celebrations and remembering birthdays. Another aspect of family work is being attentive to the emotions within a family – what sociologists call 'emotion work.' This means being attentive to the emotional tone among family members, troubleshooting, and facing problems in a constructive way. In our society, women do a disproportionate amount of this important work. If any one of these activities is performed outside the home, it is called work – management work, psychiatry, event planning, advance works – and often highly remunerated. The key point here is that most adults do two important kinds of work: market work and family work, and that both kinds of work are required to make the world go 'round. (Interview with Joan Williams. <www.mothersandmore.org>, 2000)

This pressure culminates at Christmas. Like many women, Jane remembers loving Christmas as a child and young woman. As a mother, she hates it. Suddenly on top of all the usual paid and unpaid labour, there is the additional mountain of shopping, cooking, cleaning, decorating, card writing, present wrapping, ritual phone calls, peacekeeping and emotional care taking. And then on bloody Boxing Day it all has to be cleaned up. If you want to give your mother a fabulous Christmas present just cancel the whole thing. Bah humbug!

Even at less intense times of the year, when a child is struggling with school work, the person more often at home tends to notice, worry about it and then plan a remedy. When someone in the family is unwell or worried there's a need for some action or just extra care. This concern takes a toll on mental strength just as much as physical. We often talk with women workmates about the difficulty in sometimes simply blocking out the myriad other issues we carry around in our brains when we get to our jobs. This part of the household role is always with you.

There is an awful tension between what many women in the paid workforce want to do and what they feel they ought to do. They want to earn their own money, put their skills to use, improve their status and contribute to society. But they often feel obliged to try to put others first, keep a spotless house, cook a healthy meal nightly, be endlessly and cheerfully available to their children – and husbands. This tension is behind some of the contortions women currently feel they have to perform to please everyone. It has led to a culture of self-justification. It seems almost impossible for a woman with children to say she works because she wants to. She has to rationalise her choice by claiming to do it to pay school fees, the mortgage or various other financial demands. The enormous amount of time invested in all this frantic activity is both a psychological strategy to reduce guilt about going out to work and a kind of balancing act. 'I may go to work 30 hours a week,' the harried mother seems to be saying – to herself, as much as to the rest of the world – 'but I spend at least as much time doing my womanly duty.'

And it's not as if women who are currently at home full time have it any easier psychologically. They also now feel they must justify their existence, thanks to the damaging spotlight on the largely manufactured 'mummy wars'. Perhaps this is partly the motivation that drives the anxious attention many such mothers give to their children (teachers have become particularly aware of this in recent years) and the growth in home-schooling. Again, women seem to be saying – to themselves and the world – 'I'm only staying at home so that I can protect my children from all the dangers that lie in wait for them outside.'

Personally we feel lucky to have largely escaped either of these guilt trips, give or take the occasional twinge. Why is this? Again, we don't feel we can take much credit. Instead we would offer it to our own mothers and to our feminist upbringings. Our mothers never ran around after us the way today's run around after their kids. They had a saltier, more common-sense approach to parenting, despite being full-time mothers. But there was another reason; they were both strong believers in the rights of women to fulfill their own destiny, rather than constantly worry about someone else's. And they weren't afraid to tell us so.

No wonder, as many women commute to their paid job after a hectic morning, they try to clear their heads. They need to. The workplace is no less stressful and brings its own set of very special challenges for women even after all these years, as we shall see.

6

Nine to five

When we started in our first 'serious' jobs, (after early careers as part-time checkout chicks) women were mainly congregated in junior or clerical and secretarial roles. There were few older women, and hardly any mothers around. The occasional woman in a professional or management job was an oddity and more often than not single. When one of Catherine's colleagues at a major Australian bank announced her pregnancy in the early 1980s, she also resigned. That was still the way. In the late '80s, when Jane was pregnant with her first child, she was retrenched. Twenty years later Catherine heard a similar story from a young man whose wife had been retrenched on return from maternity leave. It may be illegal but women rarely call in the lawyers because they understand that while they might win the court case, they run the risk of being tagged a trouble maker and so losing their career.

Nevertheless, today's workplaces look very different. We're all so familiar with the feminisation of offices and factories that it's easy to forget it has been one of the major social changes in the last 50 years. And the transformation is continuing. Nearly 65 per cent of working-age women are now in paid work (as we pointed out in the last chapter, many are in part-time jobs). In Australia, 76 per cent of women in the 45–54 age group are in paid work, compared with 52 per cent 20 years ago (ABS – 6105.0 - Australian Labour Market Statistics, January 2005). Some of this extraordinary flow of labour out of the home owes as much to changes in jobs and market economies as it does to feminism. There's a saying that if feminism hadn't happened in the 20th century then capitalism would have had to invent it. But this increasing participation has not eventuated in the way many of us hoped it would. Women's labour has certainly been welcomed by market economies but only on certain terms, and the norms at work, designed by and for male breadwinners still largely hold sway.

We've watched the struggles women face in trying to fit this male mould in our nearly 30 years (each) in the workplace – in supermarkets and stores, in factories, in offices and ad agencies and in the newsroom of a national newspaper. We have observed a deep sense of unease as women enter domains and ranks that were once off-limits, but don't believe this reflects a male conspiracy or genuine misogyny – although that can occasionally be the case. After all, the men we have worked with have wives, mothers, sisters and female friends. But there remains an informal feeling that women shouldn't really be there for the long haul, and as a consequence, they are not entitled to the same rewards and promotions.

Why women work

One of the surprisingly widespread assumptions about women and paid work is that they have very different reasons for being in a job than most men. For many years, Catherine has interviewed executives and CEOs from Australia's largest businesses. Time and again men in positions of power say they are puzzled by the lack of women coming through the ranks. Perhaps women just don't want the senior jobs, they say. Or they make astounding generalisations about why women work, including one CEO who assured Catherine that it was purely for financial reasons and any woman who didn't need to have a job would quit. When Catherine disagreed he was astonished and asked why women would want to be in the workplace if they didn't have to be?

For starters, many women have invested in studying or train-ing and find their job satisfying and financially rewarding. They may not want to be in a domestic sphere all the time. Jane spent five years at home with small children and remembers it as a very unhappy period. Yet society still expects women to justify their participation in paid work on financial grounds. It is seen as almost 'illicit' for women to express enjoyment of market work (Barbara Bergman, *The Economic Emergence of Women*, 1988, p. 56).

Yet women in all kinds of work have complex and varied reasons for being there. We both feel that despite all the ups and downs it was worthwhile for us intellectually and psychologically to get back into paid work after having kids. And we know many women whose motivation is much more than simply paying the bills, important as that may be. Jo, a receptionist in her late forties, who left school in Year 10, described to us how having a role outside the home was not only financially sensible but helped her feel connected to the world. After the birth of her children she continued to work part-time and while she doesn't make lots of money it's always been a priority. 'I need to do something for me and it was about getting out and keeping in the workforce,' she said.

For Jo and for us the workplace represents a very different realm from the era when our fathers went off to their jobs. In those days extended family, the community and the church exerted a powerful pull and provided social contact for the many women who remained in the suburbs. Those women are by and large no longer there. For those who remain, these changes have meant that they are more at risk, perhaps, of being bored, lonely and without effective social networks. Meanwhile jobs often now provide a kind of community, where we socialise and swap opinions, and even make friends, just like the blokes — some of whom also become our friends.

Pay gap

The level playing field was an expression once regularly quoted in the debate on women and their rights. It has largely been abandoned as it has become evident it is both an unattainable goal and a largely counterproductive concept. Even basic aims, such as equal pay for equal work, have proved remarkably difficult to achieve, despite decades of activism and lobbying. In 1998 six women employees of giant retailer WalMart launched a discrimination action against their employer alleging they had received lower wages than their male colleagues and were denied promotions.

The whistle blower who discovered her pay was lower than a man's for the same job was sacked after raising the anomaly. Her experience has led to the largest class action in the US and is still before the courts.

The pay gap data continues to alarm those who think the problem will simply resolve itself. We are often confronted with a horrified and astonished gasp whenever we quote the latest set of figures to audiences of all kinds. Research released in 2007 (by the American Association of University Women Educational Foundation) found women in the US earn less than men in the first year after they leave university.

> The study, which looked at more than 10,000 people who received bachelor's degrees in 1999–2000, found that just one year after graduation, women who are working full time earn only 80% as much as their male counterparts do.' (Juliet Rawe, *Time* magazine, 23 April 2007)

And it also found that the salary gap increases considerably over time, with women earning 69 per cent of men's salaries ten years after graduation. It's not too different in Australia where a pay gap of about six per cent exists at the end of the first year after graduation – and that's for a relatively privileged group. Australian Bureau of Statistics figures released in February 2007 show that the average full-time working woman currently earns 83.6 cents in the male dollar compared with 85 cents in February 2005. By the time young women are starting to move into their breeding years (generally in their thirties these days) the chance of retaining even their pre-children earning level is not good. This is true across the workforce – from unskilled jobs to high-end positions. In fact in 2008, new data on senior executive women showed they earn 58 per cent of the salaries earned by their male peers. The higher you go up the ladder, the larger the pay gap becomes.

This is more than unfair; it has a major impact on our society. Increasing numbers of working mothers are on their own, trying to raise a family, while growing numbers of single women, just like single men, are expected to finance their retirement. The level of their pay over their entire careers has an ongoing effect on their quality of life and superannuation – a fact that is conveniently forgotten when the mummy wars rage. This assumption that women don't need to earn the same amount as men has been around for a very long time. Decades ago, an Australian delegate to a UN forum on women listened impatiently to a presentation by conservative women about why they preferred to have a male breadwinner while they stayed home and kept house. At the end of their speech, the old warhorse of the feminist movement Betty Friedan was asked to respond. 'Well, ladies,' she said, 'that's all very well, but you are only one husband away from welfare.' This crucial reality continues to be both ignored and rejected. Despite the consistent hard stats, organisations continue to deny flatly there is a pay discrepancy between their male and female employees. Maybe it happens in other companies, they say, but not in ours. The fact that at least in Australia this difference in pay is illegal has led many women to feel this issue has been resolved.

At a forum on women and the workplace, Catherine quoted the latest pay gap data. During a chat after the presentation, a young woman lawyer became quite upset about the issue, strongly rejecting the possibility that she could be paid less than her male colleagues. 'I know I am on the same salary level as the men,' she told Catherine. 'But what about your bonus?' said an older woman listening to the conversation. The lawyer admitted she didn't know the amount of her colleagues' bonus. This is just one of the many devices used to disguise and deny the difference between what men and women are paid.

Women's work, wherever it is undertaken, is routinely undervalued and either underpaid or not paid at all. And women take this personally – they start to believe their work is of lesser quality and of lesser value.

Learning the rules

Yet young women are given very little advice about what they can expect when they start out in the workplace. Time and again young students come to Catherine's office for work experience. Enthusiastic and confident, they are looking forward to getting a job, hopefully in their chosen field of journalism. Most are doing well at school or university and they see no major obstacles in front of them. Studying hard will get them the results they need and then it will be just a matter of a lucky break to find a job and climb the ladder, most believe. The students Jane teaches at university are just as naive.

Young women come rapidly unstuck however when they realise the fellow next to them, with less experience and talent, is getting the promotion and the larger bonus – like the woman in her early thirties who told Catherine what happened in her small work team. With several years of experience as a highly capable operator Anne found out her young male colleague had continually claimed credit for work he had not done and invested much time and effort in schmoozing the boss. He was promoted over her, as she fumed from the sidelines. She was still amazed months after the event, not just at her colleague's behaviour but how the management team had been so quick to succumb to what she saw as flattery and deception. (No doubt her bosses saw a bright and promising youngster with leadership written all over him – and didn't see her at all). Anne's experience is a sobering lesson for younger women and happens all too often, even in these times when corporate rhetoric about anti-discrimination and equality of opportunity keeps on coming.

High profile businesswoman and mentor Wendy McCarthy has a theory about how the rules work against well-educated women. About 55 per cent of university graduates are now female, she points out. They are also the highest-achieving graduates, winning university medals and high marks. As a result they are sought-after employees. As young, childless women they often move through the ranks quickly, but in their thirties, many take time off to have their children. When they return, they find their male colleagues – many of whom were not as bright or as successful – have moved ahead of them, partly as a direct result of the opportunities these women created when they left. The men now have little interest in finding opportunities for the very women they once competed rather unsuccessfully against. A culture of mediocrity at the top is often the result. Indeed, another feminist friend says frequently that we'll only have true equality when there are as many mediocre women in positions of power as there are mediocre men.

Stories like this remind us all that we shouldn't automatically blame women for their failure to get ahead. We've had plenty of years watching and reading about women's lack of negotiating skill, their inability to ask for promotions and so on. We are pretty jaundiced by much of the discussion because, at best, it's a superficial reading of the systemic difficulties many women face. We don't think women need to mimic the behaviour of their male colleagues; in fact, we've seen this not just fail but backfire (more in Chapter 7). But it is clear that understanding organisational expectations and the emphasis on certain ways of operating can be illuminating, and has been revealed to us through the prism of feminism. Without feminism it is impossible to imagine that data on women and pay, women and negotiation or women and promotion would ever have been collected. We would have gone on being told that this is simply the way of the world and that women are 'naturally' less capable than men.

As a woman executive succinctly told us, 'Women are great at interviews but not so great in making an impression in a group. Blokes are better at getting the stage.' When the ground rules are second nature to you, this is not such a surprise. You only have to see how uncomfortable a man is in an all-female group to understand the difficulties many women in male-dominated environments feel all the time. They just don't articulate it in mixed company.

When Jane worked at a major international ad agency, the worldwide MD instituted a survey on why there were so few women in senior roles in the company. As one of the few female senior creatives, she was asked to participate. In her first session, Jane was unable to resist asking why the MD was asking people like her such a question, when it was the MD who actually had the power to promote. The question was brushed aside and she was quickly asked whether she felt there should be a quota for female executives. 'No,' she responded, 'but if there are no female applicants on the interview list for a position, the company should actively hunt for suitable female candidates.' At the end of the research, Jane – like the other female respondents – received a beautiful bunch of flowers from the MD thanking her for her input. These were gratefully received, but the symbolism of the gesture didn't go unnoticed. It must also be acknowledged that the company has since increased the number of women in senior roles.

What not to wear

While we have grown used to seeing women in the workplace, they have not yet shed the age-old expectations that they can be judged as much by how they look as by what they do. There are appearance penalties in many workplaces. Study after study shows attractiveness helps people get ahead in life, and in the world of paid work, where women are under extra scrutiny and often have to work harder to progress, their appearance can be the key determinant for being hired or promoted. At one of the ad agencies Jane was employed by, a senior male account director hired a PA while the managing director was on leave. The woman he selected was highly skilled and well qualified, but was also large and not very concerned about looking glamorous. On the MD's return the account director was reprimanded for hiring someone so unattractive. One of the major reasons clients liked coming to the agency, the account director was told, is because all the women who work here are beautiful and beautifully dressed.

Dowdy or overweight older women evoke a particularly unpleasant reaction, often becoming the butt of jokes or sheer rudeness if they are acknowledged at all (more about this in Chapter 7). A greying man in the workplace is often deemed experienced while a greying woman is seen as a shrew – or a witch. Every workplace has its requisite code of dress but for women there is often an added layer of expectation and concern about appearance which can feel like a burden. A few years ago at the launch of a new uniform range for ANZ employees one of the women modelling the clothes told Catherine the uniform was a terrific idea and preferable to wearing clothes from your own wardrobe because it took away all the worry she felt every morning about what to wear.

The rules about what to wear to the office, for example, have become a minefield for women who don't necessarily want to, or can't afford to, wear a suit or similarly formal attire. Dozens of wardrobe consultants now offer advice on the power dressing code needed to crack that glass ceiling (if only it were that simple). And guidance is needed – you only have to see what happens to women who wear revealing clothing to a formal workplace to realise the mixed messages about appearance are truly perplexing, particularly to younger women. Women in a range of workplaces have told us about being penalised for being too masculine or too frumpy, or for looking too sexy and distracting their male colleagues.

This can be particularly obvious when they work in the media. Women in the public eye encounter extraordinary and constant attention about their clothes and makeup that would simply be unthinkable if applied to men. Even though there's been a welcome increase in the number of women visible in the news media and in television and film roles, this scrutiny and a virtual prerequisite to look young and beautiful is as relentless as ever. Female newsreaders and journalists, no matter how experienced and capable, are castigated by viewers if their haircut or the colour of their outfit fails to please.

Sometimes just being a woman, no matter how attractive, in a male arena causes problems – as a number of high-profile scandals from the television networks indicate. In late 2007 a row erupted when Stephanie Brantz, a sports reporter at Nine, was removed from the on-air cricket commentary team amid media claims she had not 'fitted into' the bloky culture of the workplace and Australian cricketers did not want to be interviewed by her. Just a few months before, Nine was facing unfair dismissal claims after allegations concerning a return from maternity leave by another female reporter, Christine Spiteri. Not to mention the headlines that accompanied alleged comments by Eddie McGuire (former CEO of Nine) that 'Today Show' co-host Jessica Rowe should be 'boned'. There are many other examples that don't make the headlines but the rules are well understood by women in these environments, who are sent a very clear message – no matter what your skills as a journalist or actress you will be judged by harsher criteria than your male colleagues.

Career patterns

Like many of the women we speak to, Rebecca Davies, a partner and board member of Freehills law firm, loves her work. She is a senior lawyer in a leading firm and has spent many years involved in high-profile litigation work. When she joined Freehills it was not unusual for talented young lawyers to make partnership in their late twenties, which she duly did and then had her two children. She wouldn't have missed motherhood for the world. Family always comes first, she says, but she's really glad she stayed in the workplace too.

Successful men and women will both claim family comes first, but it is really only the women who are expected to do anything about it. Men may mouth the words, but – apart from rare exceptions like Tim Fischer (ex-Deputy Prime Minister), who retired to spend more time with his young children – rarely follow it up with action. Davies is happy to acknowledge that her career unfolded in a way which made it easier to incorporate childbearing whereas now young women are working very long hours over many years to achieve promotions and may find they have left their chance of motherhood until too late.

Even without this shift in the timing of partnerships, there are some other factors that are creating very serious problems in retaining women at many of the top-tier law firms. A whole cohort of women lawyers in their late twenties and early thirties are opting out, Davies said. Forget the pipeline theory, there are scores of women graduating from law school and joining firms, (up to 70 per cent of Freehill's graduate intake is women) so the numbers are there. It's what happens a few years after they enter an office and have had time to see the composition of the top echelons and the hours needed to get there that represents crunch time for many of these young women. They have to be not just smart but hard working and dedicated to even get in the door at top-tier law firms. And they work incredibly long hours to make it to senior associate. But if they decide to have a family, they still have few role models and too many question marks.

Mostly these bright young women still think about their careers as linear tracks when in reality many will end up in a cyclical pattern, taking time out for children and then returning part-time. But they also dread the mummy track. It can look like an either/or decision and some are not up for it, Davies said. Freehills have started a Corporate Mums support program to try and stem the flow. While corporate policies such as these are embryonic at the moment they do indicate something quite positive. Business is slowly being forced to realise they simply cannot afford to waste the skills, experience and talent of such a large number of potential employees. But it is foolish to expect the power brokers to suddenly experience a Damascene conversion on women's rights. If Wendy McCarthy and many other experienced women are right, fundamental change will continue to happen very slowly despite the economic imperatives of people shortages.

Workplace barriers

The term 'ideal worker' was coined to describe the norms that still underpin many workplaces:

> Good jobs typically assume an ideal worker who is willing
> and able to work for 40 years straight, taking no time
> off for childbearing or childrearing. This ideal is framed
> around men's bodies – for they need no time off for
> childbirth – and men's life patterns – for American women

still do 80% of the childcare. Not surprisingly, many
mothers find it difficult, if not impossible, to meet a
standard designed around men's bodies.' (Joan Williams
talking to Debra Levy, <www.mothersandmore.org>)

The women we work with and have interviewed over many years
will never be ideal workers and their job choices are by default
limited, even when they are highly qualified and not mothers. This
segregation of women's work operates across sectors and within
workplaces where in many organisations women are congregated
in certain jobs known as the 'female ghettoes'. This usually
includes clerical work, jobs in call centres, marketing and HR. The
Australian labour market has been particularly gender segregated,
according to Marian Baird, Associate Professor in the Discipline
of Work and Organisational Studies at Sydney University. 'We are
one of the highest occupationally sex segregated nations in the
world. That may feed into why women go not into the operations
areas, but they are in services and support. They are also the jobs
that get cut in organisations' ('Where are the women', Catherine
Fox, *AFR Boss*, September 2007).

But even before entering the workplace there is a kind of
informal streaming going on. There is very disturbing data
emerging about the job prospects of young girls who leave the
education system early. Outcomes are not good for early school
leavers of either gender, but girls are hit the hardest. In the last
25 years, while more than half the full-time jobs for teenage boys
have disappeared, an incredible two-thirds of full-time jobs for
teenage girls have simply evaporated (*The Stupid Country*, Chris
Bonnor & Jane Caro, 2007, p. 15).

For the privileged who reach university, gender still has a major impact on their choices and careers. The majority of students doing an honours degree in HR management are women, says Marian Baird, while nearly 100 per cent of students in finance management are men. Once in the workforce the culture of organisations is very male, at the shop floor, in meeting rooms and offices, and it's very hard to break that, Baird told us. Added to that, companies are asking managers to work long hours and a large part of the workforce can't do it – it's very hard to answer the phone at 2 am and look after the kids. Women doing shift work or who are on call face particular difficulties.

We've heard plenty about women getting bruised by their collisions with glass ceilings or walls or falling over glass cliffs. An industry has developed that provides advice on how to get around these barriers at work. It is catering to increasingly perplexed and annoyed women who are watching their prospects drifting away. This commercial counselling is well meaning but it is still putting the onus on women to improve by acting more like men.

Blaming women

Discrimination has become much more insidious over the last few decades.

> I think workplaces are shifting glacially. Do I see huge
> shifts or swings? No. Frankly much of the original
> discrimination or jokes or bias we saw towards women
> and people of colour or anyone who was not a
> Caucasian white male has gone underground and that's

what makes it scarier to me. (Lois Frankel, interview with Catherine Fox, 31 May 2007)

Indirect discrimination in the workplace is much harder to identify and tackle. Writer Ellen Bravo believes there are techniques that help silence women in the workplace. She says in *Taking on the Big Boys* that the 'Big Boys' rely on a series of myths to prop up the system that benefits them. One of those myths is that women only have themselves to blame if they fail to get ahead. She's even come up with a shorthand to describe the tactics powerful men use to keep women in their place. They:

Minimize – what problem?

Trivialize – that's a problem?

Patronize – You don't understand the needs of business.

Demonize – You're the problem.

Catastrophize – Your solution will cause greater problems for the very ones you want to help.

Compartmentalize – If you get what you want it will hurt some other group. (Bravo 2007, p.16)

When we talk about informal discrimination to groups of women they nod in recognition. Many find it very difficult to counter the small, niggling, corrosive attitudes and remarks they encounter on the job. And many are increasingly fed up with being lectured on techniques to counteract the constant and often unconscious belittling. They are cynical about the effects of such tactics as they have watched many women in these situations and seen very little change.

> The solution isn't just found in women thinking more
> realistically about their careers. All of our thinking,
> as solid and realistic as it might be, won't add up to
> changing a situation shaped predominantly by social
> policies, cultural inheritance, and workplaces that are still
> dominated by men. (Miriam Peskowitz, *The Truth Behind*
> *the Mummy Wars*, 2005, p.93)

The passive/aggressive workplace

In 2006, *AFR Boss* magazine hosted its annual 'Hear it From the Boss' panel discussion on leadership in Sydney. During the evening, host Adam Spencer asked guests Alison Watkins, then executive chair of Mrs Crockett's Kitchen, and David Deverall, CEO of Perpetual Ltd, about gender and leadership.

> ADAM SPENCER: Where do we stand on the gender divide
> on leadership? David, your field would be one in which
> the vast bulk of people in your position would be male?
>
> DAVID DEVERALL: Yeah. It's a really tough one. I'm a firm
> believer in just meritocracy. It's part of my generation,
> I guess. So I don't analyse the question too deeply,
> although I do recognise that when it comes to work/life

balance, stuff happens, particularly when you're in your thirties, and particularly when you're a woman, when things get really, really tough. You're raising a family and you've got the job and you're trying to balance it all together, and it's a real challenge, particularly when you're in that leadership role.

I'm blessed in the fact that I go off and work 60 or 70 hours a week and my wife doesn't and we're able to get that inbuilt balance, but it's very difficult to generalise. I certainly empathise in a big way in terms of the challenges of people-leaders, particularly in their thirties, as they start move up the executive ranks.

ADAM SPENCER: Alison, what would you say?

ALISON WATKINS: Well I'm going to be a bit controversial here but I think the view that David expressed is why we have the corporate culture that we do, and to say that it's a meritocracy and 'I don't really think about it too much' and 'I empathise', is a very passive attitude. We need a really active attitude if we want to change our workplace culture, and there's a whole lot of good sound business reasons to [exercise] positive discrimination. Taking risks with people. And I'm lucky that I've worked with a couple of men who don't sound like David ... I'm lucky I've worked with a couple of men who went out of their way to say, 'Actually, I'd like to see a woman in a leadership role. I'm going to take a risk with this woman. I know she doesn't necessarily have all the credentials, but I'm going to take a risk.' And, you know, I really wanted to make it work and they wanted to help me make it work, and it did work and as a result, they've created some change. But if we just hang back and say, 'Good women will rise to the top. Watch it happen,' it's not going to happen fast enough.

David Deverall's view is not unusual, but Watkins' response should be noted. Simply describing a workplace as a meritocracy neatly avoids addressing any of the structural problems that contribute to women's low representation. Watkins remarks drew a burst of applause from the audience, well over half of whom were women. As Jane occasionally says, when someone mounts the David Deverall merit justification, 'Define merit for me, does it involve having dangly bits between your legs?'

We have observed many women grappling with work and informal discrimination. We know they are frequently turned off applying for jobs just by the wording of an advertisement, much less recruiters who spell out to them their unsuitability for certain roles. Jane was told by a female advertising headhunter that when it came to jobs in creative departments, she was astonished by how often she was asked not to put forward any women. Women absorb the many informal signals that warn them not to venture into male-dominated or aggressive workplaces, and take note of the occasional court case brought by a woman complaining of discrimination. According to Anna McPhee, Director of Equal Opportunity for Women in the Workplace Agency, recruiters routinely tell female applicants to expect a 15 per cent lower salary than their male competitors.

Even in traditionally female-dominated workplaces like schools, women who rise to positions of power can expect to be treated differently than their male peers. At a seminar on stress and wellbeing at a 2008 conference (South Australian Women in Education Leaders Conference, February 2008), Jane was astonished to hear the female state school principals who flocked to the workshop complain – not of long hours, crowded curricula or lack of resources – but of physical intimidation and bullying by parents, particularly male parents. These women were fearful for their safety and felt they were the targets for this physical aggression precisely because they were women in leadership positions. They claimed that their male peers simply did not have to put up with the same level of threat.

Making jobs and careers work

We have worked full-time, part-time, from home, in small business and just about every other combination. The pattern reflected what options we had at the time and most importantly connected us to the workforce. That was key for us because we both knew an extended break (from advertising or journalism) was not a good move. While many people have breaks between jobs these days, women in particular continue to confront particular discrimination when they return to the workplace after kids. They find it much harder to get work, unless they return to a previous employer. It is, as we know from often-bitter experience, a gruelling path to continue full-time paid work when children are young. Some of us have no option and that's an issue that is routinely ignored.

Catherine addressed a group at a car manufacturing plant in

outer Melbourne. A surprising number of men and women turned up for the talk although one of the organisers dryly informed her that was possibly because a free lunch was on offer. At question time a few women put up their hands and then right at the end a young bloke spoke up. His wife had just returned from maternity leave to her employer and when she asked for part-time work she was sacked. He was shocked and angry. 'I didn't really get this stuff,' he said, 'but now I can see what is happening. It's really unfair.'

But returning to paid work after spending time as a mum isn't all bad news. Having kids is after all a profoundly life-changing experience and it matures you. Soon after going back into part-time employment Jane was reading the paper in her office. The managing director saw her and said, 'Haven't you got anything to do?' Without looking up she replied, 'Yes, I've got plenty to do,' and kept reading. He stood there for a moment and then left the room. Jane realised she had become both used to and confident about managing her own time.

We've both had part-time or flexible jobs and found they were a great way to blend different parts of your life, whether that involved children or household work or not. In fact, as our daughters have grown older it has been fantastic to have the latitude to write this book, for example, while continuing to earn a living.

However, many of the people we know in part-time jobs have been grudgingly accommodated and made to feel they should be grateful for the opportunity. Their pay, of course, is cut but somehow their workload rarely is, or not proportionately. Many part-time roles are nothing of the sort; they're more like full-time jobs condensed into shorter hours. And many part-timers complain about the tangible sense they are no longer part of the real workforce. They are left out of meetings and made to feel peripheral. As part-timers we have both been asked to either do without a permanent desk or share one, as if our contribution was negligible. Nothing could be further from the truth. In fact, when this happened to Jane she had just won more awards for the agency than any other writer but apparently her part-time status outweighed even this achievement.

From first-hand experience we think the part-time option challenges authority and makes managers very uneasy. Even with all the advances in technology that make remote work easier and often incredibly time-saving for those who would otherwise face a daily long commute, the idea that an employee who is not physically present is getting away with something is fixed in the minds of many. Sometimes the only way attitudes can change is first-hand experience. At a top-tier law firm a partner told us how an alpha male colleague had strenuously opposed part-time work, until a talented woman working for him wanted to switch to flexible hours. He realised he would lose her skills entirely unless he agreed. Now he's an advocate. A friend of ours job shares with her husband – they are both advertising art directors – enabling them to share the parenting of their three small children, and the ad agency they work for regards them as highly valuable employees. When Jane worked part-time for Saatchi&Saatchi the agency accommodated her shorter hours with grace and appreciation. The flexibility offered by both sides made the job the most enjoyable she ever held and the one in which she was able to perform at the absolute top of her game.

The output of part-time workers often matches that of full-timers, but in most organisations it's still an option that means immediate marginalisation. Unfortunately this is in no small part a reflection of part-time as a woman's — or mother's — path. With permanent part-time jobs still scarce, in many sectors women have been forced to look for casual work, which can be insecure, badly paid and lack basic leave and superannuation benefits. For all the talk of flexible work the progress towards a new way of organising jobs has been faltering.

Redefining work

'Why do we consider that work and family is a soft issue? We need to change the success model that is a never-at-home man to men and women working and caring together.' (The Federal Sex Discrimination Commissioner, Liz Broderick, speaking at the National Foundation for Australian Women forum Women at Work – 'the naked truth', 22 October 2007)

A woman who had recently negotiated a new job approached Catherine at a seminar on women and work. Her new employer was enormously reluctant to let her work a four-day week but she had stuck to her guns and was delighted to have started on a flexible basis. One of the sticking points in her negotiations was her request for flexibility was not to accommodate children or caring responsibilities and was therefore deemed less valid. But her skills were in such demand that she had leverage and was able to overcome the idea that a part-time role was somehow unreasonable and unearned. The skills shortage may soon see more men and women who are prepared to demand flexible work. Hopefully this will begin to remove the stigma that part-time is a special dispensation for the unambitious.

At the same time, the mismatch between paid and domestic/caring work is slowly beginning to attract more attention. But with paid maternity leave still not a reality for many women, the road ahead is looking rocky. And the problems for parents (usually mothers) trying to bridge school holidays is often overlooked. Catherine often receives feisty emails from irritated (that's putting it mildly) women trying to juggle the demands of their children with work. This one was a beauty.

> I love your columns but can't believe no one mentions the elephant in the loungeroom. For women to work and to become engaged in the economy, use their partially taxpayer funded degrees, pay tax etc, someone at a federal structural level needs to deal with the absolute, total and complete disconnect between school and work. Maternity leave, as an analyst would say, is not even in the noise of the issues women try to deal with in combining families and work.
>
> I am completely sick of it being by individual favour, as if having children was such an inconvenience and every single working woman I know has 'flexible' hours as if it were special circumstances. School has 12–13 weeks holidays, workplaces have four.

Schools finish 3–3.30, workplaces generally 5 on.

Schools have endless parent events/excursions we are expected to attend and want to attend.

Homework, as if school hours aren't enough.

Let alone children being sick.

It beggars belief no one has even raised this as a structural issue and the carry on over maternity pay continues – is it just too hard? It sure is for me.

I don't have back up as my parents have passed away so am especially sensitive to the regular parade of grandparents at the gates papering over the cracks in their children's lives and frankly being abused by the system that leaves family to fill in the gaps of a fundamentally flawed school system that is still in the 1950s.

What the hell is long service leave that I can't trade it in to try and deal with school holidays?

Where are the unions?

Where are the women politicians?

It is shredding the heads of every working woman I know.

A wealthy economy like ours should be able to have parenting packages so children do not have to choose only Mummy at home or Mummy absent.

Children have a right to be collected by their parents at least some times and to spend at least half the holidays with them – it's why most of us work at all.

I hope the workplace is kinder on my two girls than me. My friend and I successfully job-shared for over two years, with a boss happy to say so, but no recruitment agency would even consider us so we are back to trying to talk employers over the line about why we want the time not the money. Three equivalent paid days each, six weeks leave and able to collect kids from school 2.3 times a week – it's a starting point.

Please start the public discussion and stir the pot!
(Shona Guilfoyle: 19 September 2007)

Was it realistic to think the world of work would change quickly and help women to blend all these roles? That the logic or the business case for change would simply stack up and bingo – the whole system would radically alter? It may seem to us that work could be organised very differently and just as efficiently and help us stay in our jobs. But that's not how a lot of those at the top see it. Power and position and status are at stake. Women do represent competition. They want access to the top jobs and pay too. They threaten male hegemony.

Women, thanks to the F word, have made significant incursions into workplaces but their progress is at a stalemate. Feminism has alerted us to many of the problems and why they occur, but this knowledge cannot resolve the many challenges women face. The momentum for change is however growing.

The shocking pay gap figures show us this issue is not just a priority for a few but about the living standards and financial independence of half the population. And it is this topic, and the very nature of women's relationship to money, to which we now turn our attention.

7

Money matters

We are both confident debaters and public speakers. We are prepared to stick our necks out and publish opinions that we know many people vigorously disagree with and are also prepared to take the flack in response. Jane has admitted her abortion on ABC radio on a panel that included Archbishop Peter Jensen, and Catherine has served it up to academics, CEOs and business gurus from all corners of the globe. Jack Welch (famous former-CEO of General Electric) hung up on her. No one could accuse either of us of being shrinking violets or women who lack confidence. Except when it comes to talking about money. The way many of us react to money you'd think we were in danger of infection from the stuff.

There is something fundamental about the difficulty women have in their relationship with filthy lucre. Women love spending it, enjoy making it, but most hate negotiating a fair share of it for themselves. They are caught perhaps in the ancient polarisation that dictates the way men and women are 'allowed' to approach and deal with the world – men are uncomfortable with love, women are uncomfortable with money.

Not other people's money, perhaps. Women make fantastic accountants, financial advisors, bank managers, investment gurus and CFOs. As commercial lawyers women can negotiate billion dollar deals with the best of them. As long as you are not asking us to put a monetary value on ourselves we can be wheeler-dealers and high achievers, but when it comes to asking for a pay rise, most of us would rather have a pap smear. And that's saying something.

It's not easy for anyone to ask for a pay rise, but if the pay gap is any guide, almost all women find it harder or are less successful at it than almost all men. The couple of times either of us have put our hand up for more money, we've rehearsed what we were going to say for days, gone into the meeting with hearts pounding and immediately been struck dumb. We've approached it in an apologetic, so-sorry-to-be-so-demanding kind of way, handing over all our bargaining power from the outset. We can't approach it like a game, even though men say that's what it is.

To us, it's all about asking our bosses what we are worth and truth be told, however successful we may appear to be, many women have a great deal of trouble believing they are really worth very much at all. Worse, we have absorbed a message through the pores of our skin since early childhood; a message that says it is much more important that we are liked rather than valued. We are actually therefore afraid of asking for more. Terrified that our boss will tell us we're just not good enough or that even if we're successful, our less well-paid peers will get their noses out of joint. In theory, we all want equal pay for equal work; in practice, we're too afraid of losing other people's good opinion or, indeed, our job to stand up and demand it. Many women remain so grateful to have an interesting job at all the last thing on their mind is more money. And, as we'll explain, our behaviour in these negotiations is judged quite differently from that of our male colleagues.

Hard-faced bitches

These fears are not imaginary. Women who succeed in business are often seen as stereotypes: hard faced and cold. The recently deceased Leona Helmsley, who ran a very successful chain of hotels, was dubbed the Queen of Mean and vilified for behaviour that was probably common amongst men in equally-competitive endeavours. One of the only role models we can think of in business who was female and admired is Anita Roddick and not only did she work in the traditionally female area of beauty and cosmetics, but she also cloaked her brand in the language of the environment, poverty and feminism. Women, it seems, are allowed to be successful in business only if they have a higher goal than their own enrichment. No such standard applies to men.

The contradictions around financial success and perceptions of femininity are in fact increasingly well documented in academic research (and this body of data provides further evidence of why many women are failing to reach the upper echelons of organisations). There have been some fascinating studies into how deeply embedded stereotypes about gender make it so much harder for women to negotiate in an organisation, whether it's asking for a promotion or a pay rise. Studies show that women unwittingly hamper their chances of a pay rise by simply being themselves. Professor Mara Olekalns of Melbourne Business School explained to us that the ramifications are more serious than is usually acknowledged. Subtle and therefore difficult to address stereotyping issues can mean lower pay over an entire career and therefore less superannuation and less security in retirement.

And that's on top of the initial discrepancy in pay that many women will experience as they start out in their jobs. As we've already said (Chapter 6) the pay gap is firmly in place when women graduate. And on it goes, compounded by career breaks for kids and part-time work. It's well known that women in general are paid 84 per cent of the equivalent male wage, and this is often explained away as a result of women 'choosing' lower-paid occupations and working fewer hours. If that was the case, then logically one would expect women who are directly and successfully competing with men in senior executive roles would have at least narrowed that pay gap if not closed it entirely. Shockingly, the opposite is true. As we've pointed out, women in executive jobs bring home just 58 per cent of the salary their male peers do.

'The pay gap is systemic in the workplace. It's not a figment of feminists' imagination,' Anna McPhee, Director of EOWA, told Catherine when the 2007 data of the pay gap for senior women was announced. Many women still feel grateful to be in their executive roles and therefore wouldn't dream of asking for more money, she said. One woman in a top job told McPhee her boss called her in and asked if she was happy with her pay. Puzzled, the woman said she was happy and asked why her boss was inquiring. Well, he explained, all your male colleagues are constantly asking me for more money.

Rectifying the problem is not as easy as demanding more

money, Olekalns pointed out, because women who are assertive or act more like men are actually at risk of getting a poor performance appraisal because of a backlash effect. Those behaving more in line with female stereotypes – less aggressive and demanding – will fare little better in pay terms. So once again it's damned if you do and damned if you don't. Other traps for women in these kinds of negotiations, she added, include setting lower targets than men to start with, and accepting the first offer made to them instead of pushing for more.

Sometimes the 'female' way of behaving has an even more insidious effect on earnings, no matter how savvy a woman's negotiating skills. Women GPs earn between 10 and 35 per cent less than their male peers according to a 2007 study ('Female doctors earn less for giving more', by Belinda Kontominas, *Sydney Morning Herald*, 11 October 2007). The pay gap was attributed to something described as 'the tears and smears' way that women doctors tend to practise medicine. They spend longer with patients and rack up fewer consultations than men. So applying those skills usually associated with females such as empathy and listening to their job is not just unrewarded, despite demand from patients; it actually contributes to lower earnings. If that's the message women are receiving directly and indirectly in their work it must feed back into the conflict they have over identifying their own worth and feeling comfortable with translating that into dollars. So women are caught in a pincer movement, between their own internalised anxiety about money and messages from a society that doesn't attach value to either untraditional behaviour by women or, even more unfairly, traditional female skills.

Feminist analysis has helped show how this visceral disapproval of women who seek money powerfully resonates through society. Beyond the workplace, the belief persists that such women are gold diggers, out to gouge money any way they can. Free riders, if you like, selling their attractions and sexual allure to trap unwary men and fleece them (Anna Nicole Smith springs to mind.). To us, this appears to be a hangover from the days (millennia even) when the only way a woman could hope to support herself was through a man, either by marrying him, or via the largesse of her male relatives. The stigma attached to prostitution is probably partly a result of this fear of women with their own money.

It should not be forgotten that – at least in Britain, and, therefore, at that time, in Australia – it wasn't until the Married Women's Property Act in the mid-19th century that women had any right to their own money, whether earned or inherited. Prior to that, once they married, their entire worldly goods became the property of their husbands. While this law was enacted more than 150 years ago, it is worth considering that while laws may be changed quickly, attitudes can take much longer. Taught for countless generations never to ask for money directly, many women remain locked into a classic passive aggressive behaviour pattern when it comes to the subject; manipulating from a position of weakness rather than negotiating directly from a position of strength. No wonder, when as we've seen they may be penalised by the boss if they come on too strong. And of course they are often terrified they will lose their job – particularly if they are in low-paid, casual or unskilled occupations.

Divorce

This behaviour pattern is brought into stark relief by the fraught and highly emotional area that is modern separation and divorce. The often-bitter tussle over assets when a marriage breaks up is directly related to the different responsibilities that men and women still take on when they partner. Because it is still expected that women do more of the emotional caretaking, they are often the first to realise the marriage is over (as we've already pointed out most marriage break ups are instigated by the woman). This can leave the male partner feeling both blindsided emotionally, and – just to add insult to injury – ripped off financially. The bloodied and bruised male remains of such break ups often raise their voices loudest against 'militant' feminists and the supposedly female bias of the Family Court. Yet even men who have done the leaving often feel gouged by their ex-wives.

This is hardly surprising, as it is always galling to lose what you had, and any person would have to be almost super-human not to feel angry and aggrieved amid the breakdown of a marriage. Nonetheless, as we all know, men are not the most financially disadvantaged after divorce. Men whose relationships break up take a financial hit, but they have often returned to their previous financial situation within 10 years. Women, no matter what percentage of the family assets they may receive rarely recover financially, partly because their earning power is less than their husbands, but mostly because they usually retain custody and responsibility for the children. As a financial advisor once said to us, 'The best financial advice I can give anyone is that they work on their marriage.' The financial independence many women now have however has enabled more of them to leave dysfunctional marriages. This new power is both resented and feared.

Money is boring

Women are not however just poor little victims when it comes to money, and feminism has helped them realise they should take some responsibility for this blind spot. There is a tendency for women to regard conversations around money and finances as dull. Jane can certainly recall her eyes glazing over every time her and her husband's financial advisor called to discuss their affairs. It reminded her of the common dislike of mathematics that so many girls experience at school. Because so many women find the conversations about investments, interest rates and taxation et al highly technical and dry, perhaps they lazily regard it as being the intellectual equivalent of taking the bin out or mowing the lawn – men's work, and react accordingly.

This is often a fatal error and can cost women very dearly indeed. A friend endured a terrible marriage in which her husband had a barely disguised affair with his secretary for eight years. As good women sometimes do, she waited until her children were older before finally cracking and instituting divorce proceedings. The first day she saw her solicitor, the lawyer urged her to put a sheriff's order on the family business, freezing their finances. As the solicitor explained, her husband was self-employed and so much better able to hide his assets than a regular PAYE wage earner. Our friend could not bring herself to take such drastic action and as a result found herself very much disadvantaged by the eventual financial settlement. Her husband, having always taken control of the family finances, was indeed able to hide as much as a million dollars of his income and investments. Her inability to act in a way she saw as ruthless and money-grubbing has meant she will enter old age with little more than a roof over her head and a pension. He, on the other hand, has investments, houses, property, and a successful business.

Even in successful marriages, women are often woefully ignorant of their financial position and blithely so until they are left – as most women are – widows. The end result of traditional gender roles in previous generations often left the bereaved widow unable to write a cheque or the bereaved widower unable to cook a meal or operate a washing machine.

Poor old women

Financial analysts are only too aware that within the next few decades many women will be facing a financial crisis in retirement. The initial compulsory superannuation legislation failed to take into account the very different shape of women's working lives. As a result many women now in their fifties, having taken years out of the paid workforce to have and raise children, have painfully small amounts in their super. Citibank research in 2007 backs this up:

- 43% of retired Australia women aged 55+ wish they had started saving earlier for retirement
- The average monthly income for these women is $1,653 and for men is $2,455

- 56% of retired women aged 55+ say the pension is their primary source of income compared with 38% of men
- Almost half a million retired women (25%) aged 55+ years haven't started saving at all
- 36% of retired women wish they had done more financial planning.

As we pointed out earlier, women's lower pay limits how much they can put away for their old age. The fact that most women will live longer than most men compounds the looming problem. It is only relatively recently that a man's accumulated super can be taken into account in divorce settlements, no doubt a direct – if belated – response to society's recognition that we are looking forward to a generation of elderly women living on the bread line.

Even in our own relationships, our husband's super will be the major contributor to our retirement income. Yes, we have both earned more than most women do, but even the top five per cent of women earners don't come within cooee of the top five per cent of male earners. Like so many women with children we took time out while they were small and returned to work part-time. The emotional gains for doing this have been great, but the financial losses have been even greater, and this needs to be more thoroughly acknowledged. If society wants women to stay at home at least some of the time that their children are under school age, they need to make it easier and less of a financial sacrifice. Ironically, women's role as mothers may result in them becoming a financial burden to those very same children when they age.

Parenting and purse strings

It is motherhood that is really expensive for women. And that is because the hardest work in your life is not only unpaid and often taken for granted but it carries a workplace and career penalty. The repercussions for women with children in workplaces are so obvious there's a term for it — the 'maternal wall' — and there are well-documented statistics showing the impact on women's earnings from having children. If anything, says Joan Williams, pay gap statistics underestimate the extent of the problem.

> The wage gap looks only at the minority of women whose work patterns are most similar to men's, who are bound to be in better shape economically than other women. Most women's aren't. As a result, most women don't get near the glass ceiling. They are stopped, long before, by the maternal wall. ('Celebrating a Happy Equal Pay Day? Not Likely', <www.womensenews.org>, October 2002, Joan Williams)

So, working full time in the home sacrifices economic independence but mothers in the workplace are hit by a stack of informal penalties. Any enlightening discussion of women and money, we feel, must explore the connection between both realms.

Earning an income doesn't necessarily change the dynamics of economic power in the family. We know many couples where the woman is the unpaid worker of the family and most of these women believe there is no distinction or extra power attached to the breadwinner (what a loaded expression that is). We're not convinced that's entirely true, although it certainly should be. The wage earner usually has discretion over the purse strings and calls the shots in our experience, and that's not too different from when we were growing up and our mothers received housekeeping money from our fathers once a week and often struggled to stretch the budget far enough.

In fact, budgeting was very much part of the homemaker's role in those days and seemed to present few problems for women. There was little need for them to master any personal finance skills because they usually didn't have their own money or an income. Their financial wellbeing depended entirely on their husband. Indeed, such was the strange separation between women and money prior to second wave feminism, the death of the husband was not just emotionally devastating for his bereaved family; death duties often froze the family assets leaving women and children to live on the charity of friends and relatives until the taxes had been levied and the man's estate settled. When Jane was growing up a house down the road remained half built for years after just such an unexpected death.

Fewer families have such a traditional structure now because feminism brought such injustice to our attention. Modern women no longer feel they can or should rely on the financial support of one man for their survival. As a result, the surge of women into paid work, which is revolutionising our society in so many ways, is also turning attention to the value of domestic labour (see Chapter 5).

Paid v unpaid work

If women are gradually to develop a different relationship to money and engage with long-term financial planning, then this fundamental distinction between the labour of love and paid work needs to be acknowledged and reassessed. We are not really keen on the idea of a wage for those raising children and running households, mainly because no one has actually come up with a workable way of doing it. But on the other hand, it may be necessary to attach at least notional monetary value to these essential tasks to change the nature of the debate.

In fact, some estimates have already been made of the market value of household and caring labour in Australia, which was about $258 billion in 1997 (ABS, 1350.0 Australian Economic Indicators, July 2001). But those figures are based on measuring value through market replacement costs, which can only provide a vague idea of what is involved. It's impossible to put a dollar value on the role of parenting, because this is made up of what the market would call 'intangibles' – love, support and attention. But when it comes to outsourcing housekeeping and childcare, it is possible to make more accurate stabs at a total. It is predicted that over the next 20 years, $400 billion of household services including childcare will be outsourced to companies (Balancing work and family, House of Representatives Standing Committee on Family and Human Services, December 2006 report, p. 13).

Many of our friends have spent parts of their life in paid work and some periods in unpaid roles. Most of them remember being asked what they did at a social gathering and explaining they were homemakers or some similar description while watching their questioner's eyes glaze over. Work in the home carries little social cachet and leaves many men with the lurking suspicion that such women do little more than play tennis and drink coffee. (Nothing wrong with either of those activities, and we have tried to fit in as much coffee drinking and chatting as possible in our lives – but it's not all we do on our 'days off'). Work is work, whether it's paid or not, but the distinction that one type of labour is more intrinsically valuable than the other has become insidiously widespread.

Is it useful or dangerous to think of care-giving and domestic work as equivalent to market work? It's a tricky issue and one that has had feminists at loggerheads for many years. While some commentators lament the commodification and commercialisation of caring (such as US author Arlie Hochschild) and the impact of market forces on childcare, it is more crucial than ever to have an agenda for revaluing this kind of work. We don't think this is just an issue for well-educated professional women but for all women, particularly those in the casual labour force.

At least feminists are continuing to have a conversation about this, even suggesting it would be helpful if the language around work changed. As Peggy Drexler says; 'I've never liked the term: working mother. It says that I am some kind of sub-category; not a full member of the club. Maybe I'll feel better about it the day I hear someone called a 'working father.' (Peggy Drexler, *Huffington Post*, 1 September 2007) We're with Peggy on that one. Maybe an aging population will take umbrage and reframe the terms as they ease out of paid work. Maybe carers and homemakers can start pushing the point that what they do is every bit as valuable as sitting in an office.

But let's not get too far ahead of ourselves. Shaking up the attitudes to money is not about tinkering with language alone, or even obtaining superficial agreement that housework is valuable. If women are to feel comfortable and confident with financial affairs and responsibility then they will also need to unshackle themselves from the idea that they are the indispensable centre of the family. As long as women cling to this martyrdom, they will continue to believe that it's wrong and somehow unwomanly to outsource this work, and so will remain neatly trapped.

Men's haircuts, women's haircuts

Women's ambivalent relationship to money is also revealed in the way they spend. Just as women are more passive and less demanding about what they are paid (and less likely to belong to a union), so they are more passive and less demanding about what they will pay. Society may not have given us tacit permission to earn a large salary, but it certainly gives us approval to spend big. (Interesting how well each of these phenomena dovetail with the requirements of capitalism and the market.)

Shopping seems to have become the 21st century's major entertainment, and we would both plead guilty to enjoying an afternoon cruising Chatswood Chase at the drop of a hat (preferably a new one). So pleasurable is shopping now seen to be it has gained the only half-ironic name of 'retail therapy'. Women soothe themselves and bolster their egos by spending money on decorative objects, for themselves, their children and their homes. Few of us enjoy chore shopping – the regular struggle through the supermarket, or obligatory visits to banks, Medicare branches, post offices and the like, but eagerly anticipate shopping as an indulgence. Some of us become addicted to it, and the frequent stories in the media of women running up huge and unpayable credit card debts are testimony to this.

There is something pathological about the way modern women like to shop and there are probably many needs that are gaining expression through our compulsive purchasing. Certainly the virtually universal insecurity about our appearance drives women to spend bucket loads of money on beauty products we know don't work, cosmetics, clothes, shoes and our hair. Clever marketers have enabled us to buy a little bit of the glamorous lives we know we'll never really lead through perfumes, makeup and skincare products bearing the names of French couture fashion houses. Ridiculously overpriced for what they actually are, they remain nevertheless affordable and we can make ourselves feel classy and special by dabbing on a little Chanel No 5, or Dior lipstick or smoothing exotically named unguents over our aging skin. Just for a moment as we breathe in the heady fragrances we can imagine ourselves as the exotic heroines of the fanciful dreams we had about our future lives when we were little girls. A moment that only lasts as long as it takes for a child to cry or the phone to ring, of course.

It is this contrast perhaps between the reality of most women's lives and the romantic fantasies we were fed in our youth that feeds our hunger for glamorous objects. It is also this contrast that allows retailers and manufacturers to charge us so much more than they would ever dare charge a man. The classic example of this is the extraordinary price differential between men's and women's haircuts, regardless of the degree of difficulty involved in the cut. Unconsciously some of us may want these services and objects to be expensive, want them to be hard to get, and then feel guilty and wicked when we buy them because only then do they feel special and indulgent and so soothe our desire – albeit temporarily – for a pampered and indulged existence.

The push by such luxury goods companies into the male market (targeting so called metrosexuals) notwithstanding, it remains mostly women and their desire to compensate for the often-mundane reality of their lives that drives a billion dollar industry. As we keep reiterating, we are on a journey and the tug of old-fashioned femininity with its false promises of an eternal and glamorous girlhood of male admiration has not let go its hold on us (or our credit cards) yet. This is despite years of absorbing the messages of feminism that women should not be judged by their appearance and need to be liberated from this pernicious cycle of spending. What chance has feminism to be heard above the noise generated by this billion dollar industry, particularly as what the industry is selling is enjoyable, exploits our fantasies and diverts us? That's one hell of a powerful combination.

We even take this obsession with decoration and makeovers beyond our physical selves into our homes. In *Blubberland* architect Elizabeth Farrelly makes the point that women drive most home renovations. Social researcher Hugh Mackay suggests the recent explosion in home refurbishing has also acted as an escape from the real world. 'The early-century retreat into domesticity has been most powerfully symbolised by our obsession with home renovations. The quest for the perfect bathroom tile can become so engrossing, so distracting and so all consuming that larger questions – Does our government lie to us? Do we have enough to retire on? Should Australian troops be in Iraq – can't get a look in.' (Hugh Mackay, *Advance Australia ... Where?* 2007, p. 264)

This retreat from reality helps explain many women's ambivalence over money. Earning it and managing it requires that we confront reality. When we do, we discover we earn less, own less and will die with less. No wonder we'd rather distract ourselves with spending bucket loads of the stuff on bright, shiny objects, the latest fashion and anti-wrinkle cream. Much to the benefit of the peddlers of hope (and fear), feminism has become particularly demonised in this arena. It is almost painted as anti-feminine. On the contrary, we believe feminism, through such seminal texts as Naomi Wolfe's *The Beauty Myth*, has alerted us to the traps involved in conspicuous consumption driven by the fantasy that such objects will deliver the ideal you. Yet it remains equally important to remember that feminism is not anti-fun, anti-shopping or even anti-looking attractive. To us feminism is on the side of sanity and balance. It is the best protection we have against the self-defeating behaviour that plays on women's insecurities about appearance and status. This paradox around women and spending, however, reflects the complexity of the barriers to feminism. Some of these barriers are very seductive indeed, and show us how strong our insecurities are about just being female. Most women, no matter how intellectually liberated they may be, remain on some level captive to the belief that they must be attractive or alluring.

And of course there is some biological hard wiring behind that. Much as we love spending there are some things we love even more, and they are small, endlessly demanding, earth shatteringly loud and suck you dry. Literally.

8

Bringing up baby

There is a stunned look on the face of the first-time mother. We noticed it as we wandered the corridors of the maternity ward in the days after we first gave birth. Quite quickly we could tell the difference between the new mums and the old hands. Those fresh to the experience wore dazed, pained expressions, not entirely due to the physical transformation they had endured. They were in deep shock from becoming mothers. Little did they (and we) know what was in store.

But even before she comes close to giving birth, something very confronting happens to the pregnant woman. She becomes both a subject of public comment and advice, almost a communal icon, at the very same time as she turns into an alien in many formal settings – including the workplace. This is a metamorphosis that usually astonishes first-time mothers, although some have an inkling of what is ahead having watched others go through the experience. These observant women hide their condition for as long as possible in the workplace. Once the news is official however, there is a dichotomy to be faced, with happy relatives and friends congratulating the parents-to-be and perfect strangers feeling free to strike up a conversation, while the boss is muted at best. Not all bosses are like this. Jane's husband Ralph (father of two daughters who is keen on the idea of grandchildren) makes a point of rushing around the desk and giving his female employees a delighted hug when they tentatively confess to being pregnant. He believes that no amount of inconvenience at work matters in comparison to the joy of a wanted pregnancy.

We can remember how pregnancy was a time when we, and many of our friends, started to feel the artificial but pervasive push/pull of being either a childless career woman or a mother. And who could blame us? Advertising agencies and newspapers are not warm and cuddly environments. We at least partly correctly interpreted impending motherhood as a looming career problem. A problem that turned into a disaster for Jane, when she was promptly retrenched. It is true the swollen stomach can still represent an unsettling sight for many in the community and in workplaces. Pregnant women however are no longer expected to remain out of sight as much as possible or resign from their jobs, although those days are not too far behind us. Catherine was surprised by the attitude of the young obstetrician she consulted during both her pregnancies. Her only experience of doctors to that point was her GP, a woman of her own age who talked to her, not at her.

Right from the start her obstetrician had defined Catherine as a 'career woman' and lectured her about looking after the health of her unborn babies as though she was about to fling herself into toxic situations because she was too blinded with ambition and obsessed with her job to know any different. The fact he was so dedicated to his incredibly demanding medical career that he didn't see much of his own kids, as he told her, didn't seem odd to him.

When this doctor firmly recommended she give up work in the second trimester of her twin pregnancy, he meant well but Catherine couldn't persuade him that she wanted to continue working to keep her mind off how awful she was feeling and to keep some money coming in. She wanted to tell him, although she never did, that she wasn't a 'career woman'. She was a woman who had a job and children. She didn't love her job more than her children; she didn't feel they were even comparable. At a time when she felt vulnerable in every possible way, it was hard to take the implication that she was doing both the wrong thing at work (although that was never formally spelt out) and for the health of her babies. Does any father-to-be get this kind of emotional scrutiny?

Jane on the other hand had a female obstetrician who'd had two children, and her experience was entirely different. When she gave birth a second time, Jane felt something wasn't quite right with the labour. She kept apologising as she pushed, saying; 'I'm sorry, I'm sorry, but I can't get a grip, it just doesn't feel right.' Two days later, Jane's obstetrician had the sensitivity to tell her that as an experienced birthing mother her instincts had been spot on and the baby was in a posterior position (around the wrong way) and so of course it *was* hard to get a proper grip. Few who had not themselves been on the mothering end of a birth would understand just how important and empowering such a small nugget of information actually is. It is good to know that your body tells you the truth.

We are both aware from our friend's experiences that there are many wonderful and sensitive male obstetricians, but it remains a shame that the nature of the job and the nature of our expectations make it so hard for more women to become obstetricians.

Turning into a mum

The first time you give birth, you don't really give birth to just a baby. You give birth to yourself as a mother. Without wanting to belittle for a moment what it is to become a father, there is, perhaps, no greater life transition than from childless woman to mother. Perhaps that is why we so rarely hear of postnatal depression in men. The shock of this transition is blindsiding. Your body has changed beyond all recognition; it has just taken you through labour – an awe-inspiring, primeval and dangerous experience over which you have little or no rational control – and it has left you, high (but certainly not dry), weeping with the pain of engorged breasts in a hospital bed. Beside you is the world's most unfathomable creature, a mysterious newborn, that people tell you is your child.

Some women bond immediately with their child, but as any obstetrician can tell you, many don't. The more traumatic the birth, the more shocking the experience has been for them, the less energy they have to invest in the baby who after all is the direct cause of their current misery. And for many women it is miserable. Apart from the engorged breasts (an experience impossible to describe and do justice to its full horror), there are likely to be stitches to contend with, either perineal or caesarean, and if labour has been hard and long, it is perfectly possible to feel as if you have been run over by a truck. But instead of someone coming to mother you, you are expected to mother someone else. And all the eager visitors who arrive are quite clearly much more interested in the alternately squalling/comatose infant in the perspex box beside your bed than they are in you. Through it all, you are meant to be ecstatically happy and besotted with the tiny stranger that has so comprehensively invaded your body, your life and your future. Most women smile bravely and pretend, but if you look at a new mother's face carefully, as we've said, you can see how shattered she feels. The person she used to be has gone forever, and she isn't yet sure who she is supposed to replace her with.

After the birth of her second child, Jane remembers meeting one of those shell-shocked first-time mothers at some ungodly hour in the maternity ward common room of Sydney's King George V hospital. As they made themselves a cup of tea, the wan-faced and exhausted new mum said, 'Oh, well, I suppose it gets better once you go home.' Jane looked at her and debated silently whether it would be better to tell her a comforting lie or the truth and decided on the latter. 'No,' she said. 'In my experience, it gets worse. Here you've got nurses to help you, your meals delivered and your laundry done, at home, it's all up to you. All I can say is that don't think when you've patted your baby's bottom for the 682nd time at 3 am and they are still wide awake that you are the only person in the world doing it. We all struggle to get our children to do anything. And you can take comfort in the fact that in the long run, it must be worth it, because, despite everything, I am back here doing it for a second time.'

And it does get worse, at least for a short time, once you get your baby home. Firstly, many women (including us) can feel like a complete fraud as they leave the relative safety of the maternity ward pretending to be any kind of real mother. What on earth can the world be thinking of to entrust me, all on my own, to look after this very vulnerable creature? It can feel surreal the first time you are alone with your newborn at home. No state feels right. If the baby is asleep, you fear it is dead or is about to die, but you dare not disturb it to find out. If your baby is awake, you try feeding it, rocking it, taking it for a drive in the car; you try settling it, patting it, burping it, all of the 101 things everyone and anyone has told you about. At your wits' end, you put the red-faced, squalling infant in their cot and hover anxiously by the door, wondering if you are scarring your child for life by not being able to comfort it. Then the horrible thought strikes you, what if your baby simply doesn't like you? Mercifully it isn't until they are teenagers that you discover the profound truth in that observation.

And if it is terrifying coming home with one newborn, imagine how much worse it must be with two. As a mother of a toddler and newborn twins, Catherine felt as though she would never get back to a normal life again. And she didn't, but of course life did become gradually less demanding. Most mothers of twins ruefully confess that their children's first year passes in a blur of exhaustion, nappies and feeds. Catherine's twins didn't understand they should synchronise their feeding times and took it in turns to wake up every hour or so all night. Her husband dutifully got up with her to feed one of the babies and then would try to catch some sleep before going off to work. How do many families survive without a division of labour between the parents?

Catherine's premature twin daughters Evie and Antonia were

only 12 weeks old when they developed a respiratory infection and as her husband had taken their toddler to childcare in their only car she was unable to get to the family GP. Instead, she decided to walk to a local medical centre and have them examined. The woman doctor she saw was about her age and confirmed the girls would need antibiotics. As they chatted the doctor asked if Catherine was breastfeeding and she explained that despite making every effort to feed the twins, who had been failing to gain weight, she was unable to produce enough milk while also caring for a toddler. The doctor gave Catherine a severe talking to, lecturing her to pull her socks up and breastfeed them for longer or put their health at risk. There was no mention of Catherine's health, mental and physical, from attempting to care for three small children with little assistance. She walked home and collapsed in tears, feeling like a failure and incompetent at even feeding her own babies. When she told David he was furious and couldn't understand why the doctor hadn't bothered to listen when she tried to explain what she was going through. But Catherine realised the doctor couldn't see beyond those two little babies and that she was purely subsidiary to them. Catherine was no longer a person, she was a mother.

Both of Jane's children were also born prematurely: Polly at 34 weeks and Charlotte at 36. Both were also large and healthy. Jane was given steroids before Polly was induced to make sure the baby's lungs were properly developed. And thank goodness she was, because Polly caught a virus in the special care nursery of King George V, and at ten days old was admitted into Camperdown Children's Hospital with respiratory syncytial virus (RSV) positive bronchiolitis, the biggest single cause of death of babies under one.

At 13 days old, Polly had to be resuscitated three times and was given the last neonatal intensive care bed in NSW so she could be intubated and survive. Jane will never forget the intensity of fear and grief she felt at the time and also vividly recalls saying to a visitor, 'I've only known her for 13 days, but if she dies I think I will too.'

Every mother has a story about the dawning realisation that they are no longer an autonomous individual; some of those stories more extreme than others. Motherhood is not like any ordinary job, it is not something you can pick up and put down. Women who secretly find themselves occasionally resenting this demanding new presence in their lives are neither unnatural nor unusual. They are simply normal. This needs to be acknowledged, not ignored. However much we love our children, none of us can give up our autonomy without some grief over the loss.

Crucially, acknowledging the real − rather than the romanticised − experience of mothering is essential if we want to help and support new mothers adjust. Feminism has enabled us to bring the experience of pregnancy and childbirth out of the closet, because it has legitimised such experiences and challenged the belief that women are naturally equipped to deal with them. When our own mothers gave birth to us, they had little access to information about what to expect in the labour ward or the nursery. If they asked, they were often dismissed or told to shut up. Now the opposite is the case, whole sections of bookshops are dedicated to pregnancy, birth and parenting. It ain't secret women's business anymore.

Solitary confinement

Like the heady madness of romantic love, mother love is hardwired into us to ensure the preservation of the species. The female of the species carries the brunt of this biological imperative. We are not crying out for sympathy here or painting mothers as martyrs and victims. There are tremendous rewards in motherhood, profound discoveries about yourself, your children and the nature of life itself that probably cannot be understood any other way. But the sweetness of your babies' smiles and laughter, the privilege of the trust such a vulnerable creature places in you, the demanding but unswerving love they give you in return, still comes at a price. Motherhood, like anything else worthwhile, is hard and the joys are often fleeting and hemmed in by drudgery, exhaustion and lack of support. We just wonder why our social system has to make something as vital as mothering even harder.

The loneliness of new motherhood really shocked us. Unrealistically, we'd imagined the first few months at home with a baby would be spent catching up with friends and getting to do all the things we assumed people did when they didn't rush off to a paid job every day. But mothering is of course a job, it's full-time and more and takes up nearly every second of the day, unless the baby is asleep, at which point you lie down to get some rest yourself. Windows of opportunity for seeing friends or colleagues were limited, and suddenly that group of new mums we had just met at mother's group became our best friends because they were going through the same nighttime feeds and mastitis crises as we were. You could shoot a cannon down the middle of most suburban streets these days and not hit a thing, apart from the odd lorikeet. The isolation can be terrifying. No wonder there are so many social problems in areas of low-cost housing on urban fringes, where new mothers are often stranded without a car or regular public transport.

And then we wonder why so many new mothers suffer the agonies of postnatal depression. Meeting other mothers was essential to help us weather those first few months. We interviewed a number of women about their feelings at this crucial time and most found their mother's group an enormous support as Fiona, the mother of two girls (9 and 14), describes:

> Mother's group was the best thing. In fact I still have two or three people I see from then. It was the support and it was my outing, some socialising. And seeing people. Otherwise you felt like all you were doing was looking after the baby and waiting for your husband to come home, it was for your own sanity and it made you enjoy motherhood.

There's still a surprising taboo around admitting that mothering isn't a barrel of laughs. When Helen Kirwan-Taylor of the London *Daily Mail* wrote about how boring raising children can be she unleashed a furious international public reaction. The blogosphere went into meltdown, she received worldwide publicity and was interviewed extensively in the media. Reactions ranged from 'good for her for telling the truth' to 'she's a selfish, spoilt bitch who doesn't deserve kids'. The heat generated by her article reveals the extreme discomfort felt when women refuse to live up to the stereotype of mothers that we all hold so dear. Such honesty may also remind us uncomfortably about the way so many of us exploited our own mothers when we were young. Children don't want to hear that their mother may have occasionally resented them and their demands, or that sometimes, in the dead of night, she may even have wished she'd never had them. We are all someone's children.

But the uncomfortable truth remains that the traditional stereotype is no longer remotely typical. The reality is that most first-time mothers have left a job of some sort. This understandably leads them to attempt to apply the same organisational techniques they'd use in the workplace to a baby. It's not unusual to hear the language of efficiency and speed used to measure the level of achievement reached by their child. Some of the new mums in our mother's groups proudly talked about how quickly they'd returned to their pre-pregnancy weight, how many hours their babies would sleep or later on, how quickly the toilet training was progressing. The baby health booklet, where you record your child's health details, becomes the equivalent of the annual KPI discussion. This competitive view of good mother/bad mother is deeply intimidating for the insecure, inexperienced first time mother, and that's all of us. Most mothers have no training or guidance when they set out on this journey and it takes a while for any new mother to realise that the role is not innate and often represents a trial for many women, especially if they embark on motherhood with high expectations and so become ashamed if they are not instantly successful.

Salvaging yourself

Even though motherhood changes a woman profoundly, she still remains more than her parenting role. The risk perhaps in motherhood is the temptation to lose yourself and give up all the things that used to define you. It is a common experience at parenting assistance centres such as Tresillian for the nurses and counsellors to find that many of the mothers they are helping have completely stopped doing anything for themselves – to an unhealthy extent. However, the buzzword in parenting these days seems to be the need to bring up a 'resilient' child. A child who is not always happy or sheltered from any of life's inevitable difficulties and dangers, but who has the inner resources to get through whatever life throws up at them. It would seem to us therefore that the first prerequisite for a resilient child is a resilient mother. And turning oneself into a martyr or a self-sacrificing saint is unlikely to create the necessary strength.

Indeed, in the doormat myth of motherhood the fundamental aim of child rearing appears to be forgotten. As a counsellor who worked with children and grief once explained: 'The job of a child is to grow up'. In other words, the child's task from the moment they leave the womb is to separate from the mother and to create their own independent life and identity. The cliché of the clingy, needy, manipulative monster mother is perhaps the inevitable result of a mother who no longer has her own separate identity.

By encouraging women to see themselves as more than wives and mothers – as workers, voters, citizens, artists, writers, politicians, managing directors, business operators et al – feminism has offered a powerful helping hand to the child as well as the mother. But that's not all. The F word, contrary to much popular opinion, has also it seems to us profoundly changed and improved fatherhood.

Dads

When we were born, back in the 1950s, our fathers were only peripherally involved in the event. While modern day men who hold grudges against their ex-wives often like to refer to themselves self-pityingly as 'sperm donors', it seems to us that such a term was a much better fit for our father's generation. They were excluded from the labour and birth, left hanging around bars and waiting rooms to be told the result. There has been some discussion of the consequences of fathers being present at the birth of their children in recent years. Some psychologists claim that the experience can be traumatic and that for some men seeing their wives in labour can make it difficult to find them sexually attractive again post-birth.

As women who have been through labour we can't help choking a little at the idea that merely watching could be labelled a trauma. The deterioration in sexual attraction we know less about, as neither of our own husbands seemed to find any difficulty in relating to us sexually after watching their own children being born. Jane's husband turned into something of a post-birth bore for a few years, waxing lyrical to any who would listen about how fantastic and miraculous the whole process was. Our own experience is that having our husbands be part of labour and birth bound us more closely with them and helped them bond with their daughters more profoundly and quickly. It also – and this is no small thing – increased their respect for us. They saw what we had gone through and how we had handled it and they were impressed.

In the previous generation our fathers were also largely excluded from a leading role in parenting. This was sad because they suffered a loss and so did their children. As the oldest of four, Jane has only one memory of spending any real time alone with her father as a child. It was during a family holiday in Surfers Paradise, when her three younger siblings came down with a nasty dose of flu and had to be cared for round the clock by her mother. Judged a disastrous holiday by everyone else, Jane remembers it as a golden time, when she and her father spent days and days in one another's company. It was the novelty of this experience that gave it its special charm.

Catherine's father was unusual for his generation and couldn't get enough of his four babies, often holding them and helping her mother with night-time burping sessions after they were fed. He took immense delight in his kids and every silly thing his children said, which he repeated for years (and years and *years*). Of course, as with Jane's father, as the sole breadwinner he was not around as much as Mum as the children grew up and therefore had less involvement than today's fathers in many aspects of parenting. He would have been delighted to do more had time and the social mores of the era allowed.

Twenty years ago, around the time our first children were born, it was common for men to be at the birth and this seemed to lead them to want to be more involved in hands on parenting than their own fathers had been. But there was still a slight unease around this, as if the parenting work itself would somehow 'unman' them. Some fathers still made nasty tasteless jokes about how they'd avoided having to change any more nappies by deliberately sticking a pin in their baby the first time. Yes, some babies still wore cloth nappies back then. While we were never terribly convinced by this macho boasting, it is impossible to believe that any father could actually do such a thing to a tiny baby on purpose; the fact that such a lame joke could still raise a burst of boisterous male laughter indicated we still had a way to go. From our observation of new parents today, that ground has well and truly been traversed. Men simply do not make the fuss they used to make about changing nappies any more. It is no longer a big deal, thanks to feminism – and disposables.

Today, if you see families out for a stroll, Dad pushes the baby. This is revolutionary. Even better, it is now common to see fathers out and about in sole care of even the tiniest newborns. Fathers and children are everywhere – at sporting venues, in shopping centres, in restaurants. Some of them are divorced fathers during weekend access visits, but many of them are not. Many of them are the lucky beneficiaries of a feminism that gave their wives permission to say, 'You take the baby this morning; I want some time to myself.' Something our mothers, despite their strength of character and outspoken personalities, would simply never have dreamed of saying when we were small. This not only gives mothers a chance to reconnect with their essential and separate selves, it also gives fathers a chance to get to know their children in the only way that really works, and that is by actually looking after and caring for them.

Nevertheless, in our own lives we have seen and experienced the dilemmas that have also been created for both fathers and mothers by these changes. One of them is the development of a kind of competition between the two parents. Once, work in the home was clearly divided; if it was inside the house or involved the children, it was her job. If outside, it was his. Now, it is not so clearly delineated. While a marriage remains happy, this probably doesn't matter so much, but once it deteriorates it can lead to all sorts of bitterness and anger. The phenomenon of the angry and aggrieved divorced father is probably a direct result of the new relationship that is now forged between fathers and their children. It is probably much more of a grievous blow for a modern father to lose day-to-day contact with his children than it would have been for fathers of previous generations. Not because they didn't love their children as much, but because they didn't see them as much.

Parental choice

Motherhood itself, thanks to the increased involvement of fathers, has become more rewarding for women, we believe, but it remains hard and relentless work for at least 20 years. After having weathered babies, toddlers, school children and teenagers, our view now is that the cumulative degree of difficulty doesn't change, it's simply what is difficult that does. For example, with babies it is the continual yet unpredictable nature of the work of mothering that is so exhausting. As one experienced mother put it, 'With a new baby the only advice I can give you is not to expect today to be anything like yesterday or tomorrow to be anything like today.' It is hard – physically hard – to be a life support system for another human being.

As children grow and become more physically capable and therefore less physically demanding, their parenting becomes more emotionally, psychologically and intellectually challenging. Because our generation is having fewer children than previous generations – we are both one of four – and we have far more money to spend on them, parents also suffer the agonies of an excess of parental choice.

If you think we exaggerate, let's just take a look at some of the choices that face today's parents, particularly mothers. Firstly, our generation has much more choice about whether or not we want to be parents at all and, as the continual increase in the age of first-time mothers shows, spend years deciding. So long, in fact, that by the time we decide, our fertility has often declined to such a point many of us must then choose whether to let nature take its course, or embark on the emotional rollercoaster that is fertility treatment.

There is a bewildering array of choices surrounding the modern process of giving birth, and things only become more stressful and confusing once the child emerges. Will you breastfeed and for how long? Will the baby sleep in your bed or in its own? Will you leave it to cry or rush to comfort? Will you feed on demand or on schedule? When will you give solids? Is a non-organic carrot going to give it cancer? Cloth nappies or disposables? Canned baby food or homemade? Vegetarian or omnivore? Will you immunise or not? When should you potty train, leave baby with a sitter, and the big one; when should you go back to work? And for all these choices there are a thousand providers of their opinions, all different, all plausible, all sure they are right. Then as the child grows, if you do go back into the workforce or even if not, what sort of childcare do you choose or can you afford? Expensive and private – a nanny, perhaps? Long day care, occasional day care, family day care, the lady next door, or like many parents, a cobbled together schedule of grandparents, neighbours and paid care?

The lack of formal childcare options is not a new problem in Australia, with affordable care an enormous dilemma for many parents, particularly those in lower-paid jobs. Most children up to the age of two who are in care are being looked after by family, friends, babysitters or a nanny, but by the age of two nearly half the children in Australia are in formal care. ('Balancing Work and Family', House of Representatives Standing Committee on Family and Human Services report, December 2006)

Whether your child is in childcare or not, the unending list of choices continues. Do you hothouse? Do you restrict TV, spend hours with flashcards, get them into kindy gym, toddler's music lessons or baby ballet? Or let them run around the backyard with their nappies off playing in the mud, while you watch from the sidelines with a well-earned glass of cask white?

Eventually, they are old enough for school, and this is where the big guns that influence parental choice really start to make their presence felt. Will you send them to the public school down the road, or to the prestigious prep school the girls at mothers' group are sending their kids to? What about Montessori, Catholic, Jewish or fundamentalist Christian? Or will you home school? And will you start after-school coaching and when? How young is too young for Suzuki method or Kumon? And if you choose not to send them, because they already kick up something fierce about swimming lessons and ballet and little athletics and they do have rather nasty black circles under their eyes, will they be disadvantaged? Are they – oh, horror of horrors – in danger of being Left Behind?

But parental choice hasn't finished with you yet. In fact as your children grow older, the choices broaden and often become more fraught; there are schools, drugs, boyfriends, parties, alcohol and, of course, sex to contend with. You get the picture. The management work of parenting simply never stops, particularly – as the media are telling us – they now don't leave home. As we've pointed out, it is insidious how standards keep being ratcheted up and parenting is no exception. This generation of parents, particularly those in the middle class, have put unprecedented pressure on themselves and their children to comply with unrealistic standards of perfection in achievement, behaviour, appearance and endeavour. Kids can't just be kids anymore; they have turned into little advertisements for their parents. A scruffy, underachieving child can't be laughed over anymore; they've become a reflection on their mother's (lack of) ability as a parent. There is even a 21st-century phenomenon of the middle class mother (never the father) quitting her job to get her kid through their final school year.

Bad mothers

The pressure on married women to be perfect mothers is oppressive but on single mothers it is untenable. They can't win a trick. They have 'deprived' their children of a father figure and bizarrely are often seen as bludgers; there is a particular tendency to disparage them for reliance on social security. How anyone could imagine bringing up kids on your own is a cushy number is beyond us. Nevertheless, single women were singled out by punitive welfare policy under the Howard government. While married women were tacitly encouraged by tax policy to stay at home, single mothers were literally forced to return to the workforce when their youngest child turned six. At the time, stories quickly emerged of such women being expected to travel long distances for poorly paid, insecure and unskilled work regardless of their caring responsibilities. But in the 2007 Federal election, according to George Megalogenis, these women had their revenge. Electorates where single parents were represented in large numbers swung to the ALP. Community services Minister Mal Brough lost his seat. Contrary to the rather smug assumptions of some policy makers, these women are neither marginalised nor cowed; they're angry and they're standing up for their kids.

And that's the thing about mothering. For all the work and angst they cause us, we are fierce about our children. In fact, if society wants to improve the outcomes for young people, as feminism has long been saying, the first thing it should do is support mothers. Honestly, if any of us really understood what we were letting ourselves in for when we decided to have children, would we ever do it? Well, yes we would, because while it is much harder to describe the joys of having children than the grief, those delights are very real. After almost two decades of parenting, there is, however, one thing that drives both of us to screaming point, and that is the tendency for all sorts of people, but particularly those who do not take the same hands on responsibility for raising children that mothers do, to say about any and all delinquent behaviour; 'I blame the parents', or 'Where were the parents?' or 'Their parents should do something.'

We parents are doing something, just about all we can in most cases but still we find little support or even acknowledgment for the enormous task we have taken on. The trouble with parenting is that we all start out believing that we are going to be fabulous and, if we are honest with ourselves, end up realising we've been just as crap as all the parents who have gone before us – our hearts go out to the parents of 2008 teenage media bad-boy Corey Worthington. That's why nothing makes you re-evaluate your own parents better than becoming one yourself.

At least, when there are two parents involved, you can share the sense of bewilderment at the latest teenage outrage. Marriage may not be the important institution it once was, as we are about to examine, but a supportive partnership of some sort while raising a family can be sanity saving.

9

Love, sex and marriage

Paradoxically, it is often the experience of marriage and childbearing and rearing that radicalises many women despite the enduring myth that just the opposite occurs. For this is the life stage when the true consequences of our gender and biology really begin to bite (as we examined in detail in the previous chapter). The Faustian bargain that society has traditionally offered young women involves trading romantic love and sex for the protection and economic support they need via a husband who will negotiate the wider world for them. And for a while, that almost seems plausible – even today. But when the full impact of what is expected of women as they move into this phase of their life emerges the inequities soon become apparent.

In the first flush of love and partnering, feminism can seem irrelevant, even perhaps threatening. Maybe this helps to explain why most young women today no longer identify as feminists. Mind you, there is nothing new in this. Young women have generally not strongly identified as feminists, and didn't even when we were young, in the so-called hey day of second-wave feminism. It often has little immediate attraction to them at this stage of their lives. While young, many women have a narrow kind of power, but a power that is none the less potent. Very quickly, as they change from children into teenagers, many young women begin to draw a disproportionate amount of male attention. Even those who are not necessarily recognised as beautiful are often at their most attractive between the ages of 15 and 25, and there is clearly some kind of biological hard wiring that causes men — of all ages — to be particularly drawn to young women in their prime fertile years. For many, this attention becomes so constant, so much a part of everyday life, that they cease to be conscious of it.

Jane remembers pushing her first baby in a stroller past a building site and being absolutely astonished by the silence that greeted her journey. It was the kind of silence that on film would have been emphasised with the chirruping of crickets and tumbleweed blowing past. Whistling, shouts and exaggerated sexual responses had become part of her expectation of building sites, and while she tensed on approach and claimed to find the attention both unwanted and embarrassing, a chill stole over her as she walked through the quiet. Something fundamental about her relationship with the world had changed, and changed forever. A power she once took for granted — perhaps even claimed to despise — had left her, and she realised she was going to miss it.

More recently, at 50, she travelled overseas with her 16- and 19-year-old daughters to discover she had become almost entirely invisible. Her mother then cheered her up by warning that it only gets worse, remembering that when she let her hair go to its natural white at 65, she completely disappeared.

The illusion of beauty

It is, we believe, the sweetness of the attention women receive from men when young and the confidence in the power that this attention brings which makes so many young women believe that sexism is not an issue for them. The world really is theirs for the taking they think, and simply by batting their eyelids (employing the so-called feminine wiles) they will always be able to get what they want. Given that nothing about human responses – particularly subconscious ones – is ever simple however it is also worth remembering that the power that comes with physical appearance has long been a double-edged sword for young women. The impact of their sexual allure is why women are so brutally repressed in some cultures (see Chapter 10) and why affluent young women in the West are so obsessed with their looks and so easily fall prey to eating disorders. It also seems to be why women – especially beautiful women – rarely allow themselves to take pleasure in their appearance. On the contrary, so important is women's appearance they are almost universally hypercritical of themselves.

No matter how thin we are, we are not thin enough; no matter how beautiful, we focus on our imperfections; no matter how shapely, our hips, our thighs, our tits are always either too big or too small. This endemic insecurity quite understandably drives the men in our lives crazy. Women's dependence on their sexual attractiveness frightens us, because we recognise its importance but also understand it is accidental – the result of good genes rather than good management – and temporary. Like the athlete, the beautiful woman has a short shelf life.

But for some women, skill with feminine wiles, more perhaps than conventional beauty alone, has brought ongoing power, or at least a close relationship with power. In recent times, socially prominent women such as Pamela Digby-Churchill-Hayward-Harriman and Jacqueline Bouvier-Kennedy-Onassis probably exemplify the more traditional path women took to gain power and influence, by seducing and marrying men who had it. But even these women were profoundly changed by ageing and by feminism. Pamela Harriman ended her life as the pre-eminent fundraiser for the American Democrat party and the US Ambassador to France. Jackie Onassis built a solid reputation for herself as a book editor and publisher.

Generally however women's power wanes as they age, because they simply no longer attract men. Perhaps this is why ageing Western women resort in ever-increasing numbers to the self-mutilation we call cosmetic surgery. The male experience is often just the opposite. For some, their power increases as they age, allowing the more successful to trade in the old wife for a younger and sexier model. Rupert Murdoch dumped an ageing wife for the young Anna Torv, then proceeded to dump an ageing Anna for the youthful Wendy Deng. But you don't have to mix in such exclusive circles to experience humiliation and betrayal. We will all age, and despite the billions poured into lotions, potions, creams, botox, chemical peels and cosmetic surgery, a 40 year old will never be able to compete on the sexuality index with an 18 year old.

The loss of beauty

Prior to the resurgence of feminism in the 1970s, the ageing process certainly seemed particularly bleak for women. Women dreaded ageing; over-painted and bleached movie stars past their prime were held up as awful warnings. Women over a certain age were expected to meekly accept their fate and retire gracefully. Those who refused were mercilessly held up to ridicule. Plays and films in the 1950s seemed to delight in a kind of prurient disapproval of dipsomaniac older women clinging pathetically to their youth by attaching themselves to a pretty young man on the make. Examples of this genre include Tennessee Williams' *Sweet Bird of Youth* (Geraldine Page and Paul Newman) and the Gloria Swanson–William Holden coupling in *Sunset Boulevard*. Considered very daring and quite shocking at the time, both look, thank goodness, very dated today. Thanks to feminism and no doubt the increased spending power of ageing baby boomer women, this attitude is now less apparent. Jane Fonda – always on the cutting edge of women's rights – spruiks skin care products by boasting about her 70 years, something no movie star worth her salt would have done a few decades ago. These days, some women are even confident enough to joke about their own struggle with ageing, sending up their own physical appearance. Nora Ephron writes:

> Every so often I read a book about age, and whoever's
> writing it says it's great to be old. It's great to be wise
> and sage and mellow; it's great to be at the point
> where you understand just what matters in life. I can't

stand people who say things like this. What can they be thinking? Don't they have necks? (Ephron 2006, p.18)

And Ephron then goes on to make a good point about age and appearance: the 'reason why forty, fifty, and sixty don't look the way they used to [is] not because of feminism, or better living through exercise. It's because of hair dye.'

Despite some signs of change however society continues in its attempts to dismiss older women, and post-menopause, women are often seen as relatively useless because they are no longer either sexually attractive or fertile. But these days older women are refusing to be so easily ignored. It was not young or single women who led the revival of feminism in the 1960s. Betty Friedan's famous 'problem with no name' was the complaint of the married housewife with schoolkids, locked into the 'burbs. Educated women felt a promise had been broken when they took on the role of compliant housewife and mother. Contrary to cultural expectations, many didn't feel happy and satisfied in their homes; they felt trapped, powerless, trivial, despised and invisible. One of the great furphies about feminism is that it devalued housewives and mothers. This was not the case and could only ever be true if such women had ever enjoyed high status previously.

A woman who was a housewife and mother in the 1950s tells a pointed story about the double standard that was in full swing at the time. A man was holding forth at a dinner party about why women could never be equal to men because women were in fact naturally superior. He waxed lyrical for a while about women's pure and ethereal nature and their special status as objects of worship and romance that needed to be both venerated and protected. Irritated beyond endurance by this pontificating, our friend interrupted him by saying; 'If that's so, if women are so precious and special, how come it's always us that get down on our knees and scrub the toilet?' Housewives and mothers have never gained status or even recognition, in any society. But for many centuries, low status or not, to be a mother of sons (pity the woman with only daughters) was as good as it was ever going to get.

Walking up the aisle

Even today, marriage remains one of the most recognised ways women can gain higher social standing. This may explain the renewed obsession with changing maiden names on marriage. Marriage certainly changed us, but not our names. After nine years of living together, Jane was surprised by the emotional impact of changing from a partner to a wife. She thought she was getting married because she wanted to have children. Looking back, she now sees there was a sense of safety and security and commitment that perhaps hadn't been expressed or felt so powerfully before. A pessimist by nature, Jane had only managed to get herself down the aisle (actually it was the lawn of her parent's garden) by repeating over and over to herself, 'I can always get a divorce, I can always get a divorce.' Twenty-three contented years later, the need to get that divorce still hasn't arisen. Despite this however she remains true to her bedrock pessimism. 'Never say never,' she says.

Meanwhile Catherine was pretty much resigned to life as a singleton until she reconnected with David on returning from two years working in London. Although the marriage proposal followed a typical rant from Catherine about not waiting around for him to make up his mind while her body clock ticked on, it's safe to say the union was actually a joint decision. And looking back, she is grateful for the strong biological urge to have children which suddenly and unexpectedly hit in her early thirties. Never one to pick up the baby or cuddle the toddler at a family gathering, Catherine was overtaken by a real yearning for a child, and marriage therefore made a lot of sense. But the thought of changing her name (as we examine later), or spending weeks choosing a wedding dress, or wearing a garter to rip off and throw to the crowd horrified her. It all seemed so silly. Jane and Ralph, on the other hand, really pushed the boat out – with bridesmaids, groomsmen, the full bridal catastrophe, but with a celebrant rather than a priest. In the end, Catherine and David's wedding was held in a church (at her parents' request) and a reception followed. But the trimmings were kept to a minimum and while it was fun there were no expectations that this would be the most important day of their lives. And if pushed, both Catherine and David were too pragmatic to rule out the vague possibility it might not last forever.

After all, 40 per cent of first marriages and 60 per cent of second marriages end in divorce. As recently as our own mothers' generation, an unhappy marriage could be a prison for a woman. It was a situation she was forced to remain in regardless of the misery she experienced, because of her children and her lack of financial alternatives. And it made no difference whether this included active violence and abuse or was simply the misery of two mismatched personalities chafing against each other. Wives and husbands were expected to put up with their lot.

Feminism has helped women gain the financial power and inner confidence they need to leave such relationships. While this has no doubt caused much pain, it must not be forgotten that it has also alleviated a lot of it too. Critics who believe feminism has gone too far and caused a modern epidemic of family breakdown forget the enormous cost many women paid to remain in their marriages. If the only way a family can survive is by limiting the freedom and potential for happiness of one of its members (often the woman) then there is something wrong with the way the family has been set up. A system has to work well for all its members before it can be considered successful.

We recognise just how fortunate we have been. Indeed, it may be worth taking a moment to look at why our marriages have lasted − at least until the time of writing. Neither of us would claim we haven't had rocky patches, the worst probably when our children were small, but somehow we have survived them, when many other couples have not. How? Is there a secret? Are we in some way special? These are questions we are frequently asked, so we will attempt to answer them here, but the last thing we want to do is create the impression of being a pair of smug marrieds. The longevity of our relationships is almost as much of a cause of bemused surprise to us as it probably is to others. Remember, we both went down the aisle under no romantic illusions of lasting happiness. When Jane and Ralph first got together, for example, back in 1975, close friends gave them six weeks!

An old friend who has also been married for over 30 years once suggested that the secret behind successful modern partnerships is that the distribution of power between the couple − even though it inevitably ebbs and flows at various periods − is more or less equal. We have no proof of this, but looking at our own marriages, and those of our friends in similar circumstances, it seems to make sense.

However, we both feel that the majority of the credit probably lies with our own parents' successful and supportive relationships. Perhaps we just absorbed some of the skills needed to maintain a good marriage simply by being such close observers and lucky beneficiaries of our parents' skill and wisdom. This is not to say that the children of divorced parents, or of intact but unhappy partnerships cannot forge successful marriages. Obviously they can and they do. Indeed, they deserve real credit for doing so, having obviously learnt from their parent's mistakes. The difference is that we probably do not deserve such credit. We fully recognise we have been lucky rather than wise. Both of us give particular credit to our fathers. Andrew and John both lived up to the old saying that the most important thing a man can do for his children is to love their mother. This was a great gift to both of us.

It is impossible to exaggerate the importance a supportive, loving and loyal partner has for a feminist, or indeed for anyone trying to live their life in a relatively new and untried way. And, without wanting to discount the value of same sex partnerships, we would both also acknowledge that having a male ally − a friend in the other camp, if you like − has been a godsend, particularly when we have felt bewildered, insecure and under attack.

Such a sympathetic partner can translate 'male-speak', particularly when a woman is unsettled by a bewildering and unclear conversation with a male colleague or superior. Forget the 'men are from Mars, women are from Venus' school of male/female relations; but our own life experiences have shown us, not to mention all the recent research proving the fact beyond doubt, that while women and men are humans first and gendered second, we do often respond to the world differently and use different modes of expression to communicate. This can and does lead to confusion and hurt feelings, and is why men who genuinely like and feel comfortable around women (as opposed to just enjoying having sex with them) are so important as friends, mentors, allies and of course partners. But we strongly believe that a successful partnership is about having equal input and power, not the domination of one over the other. Which is why we have long been fascinated by the symbolism of changing surnames on marriage.

It's all in the name

Whenever anyone pooh-poohs politically correct language it's usually time to watch out for some hypocrisy. Critics of political correctness often mention how trivial and ridiculous it is to alter and de-gender language to symbolise the shift in our society. It doesn't matter, they say. But then, if you are the person in power, who is routinely deferred to and automatically included in everyday language, then the experience of being marginalised or not even mentioned is alien to you. And when the powerful are inadvertently excluded, these critics may also find the experience unpleasant. In keeping with this fashionable scorn about political correctness is that one of the most ridiculed terms of recent times has been the use of Ms as a female version of Mr. The logic behind the term of course is simply to provide a title for women that doesn't denote marital status.

The fraught distinction of being a Mrs, Miss or a Ms is endlessly irritating. Catherine's sister Geraldine has been lectured by a young man taking down her details about the nuisance she causes by insisting on using Ms. This is clearly not a question that men have to contend with because presumably their marital status is irrelevant. In fact, the title itself seems to symbolise a feminist troublemaker to many, and these reactions would indicate its use is far from trivial. And they come from both men and women. The fuss made about it signals something much more disturbing is going on.

Perhaps it's because marriage and the whole idea of 'catching a man' remains a holy grail for some women who believe it awards them higher status than their unmarried sisters. It seems to us that changing your name on marriage is a particularly tenacious hangover from much earlier times when women literally became their husband's legal property in matrimony. In fact, such symbolism is precisely why we didn't even consider changing our surnames, along with the sheer work involved in changing every piece of personal identification, plus bank accounts and driving licences.

We felt that our names were an intrinsic part of us – our formal identity. We simply couldn't imagine altering that and even now, when the topic comes up for discussion, the notion that changing your name shows you love someone seems peculiar to us. Why do you need to change your name to demonstrate that? And if that is the case, then why do women change their names and not men? The practical aspect of what surname to use for the children is often trotted out as another reason for name changing but that's a rationalisation too. Jane's children have her husband's surname and it has never been an issue. Catherine's have a hyphenated surname and that hasn't proved inconvenient either. Changing your name to your husband's also denotes an absorption into his identity. An extreme example of this was the late Princess Diana, who of course should never actually have been called by that name. Her official title was Princess Charles, but it was never used. The public simply wouldn't wear it – and nor, it seems, would she. Princess Michael of Kent, on the other hand, does not seem to be made of such stern stuff.

This is a social custom which in many ways has lost its meaning but still taps into a deeply emotional notion of romantic love and marriage. Several women we spoke to while researching this book remarked on the number of younger women they knew who were determined to change their names. They speculated there was still a level of informal pressure that is all about social convention. Like the handful of our own friends who still promised to 'obey' at the altar, this passivity worries us. It seems to us an indicator of a woman who is so caught up with the romantic notion of being a bride that she has entirely forgotten what the harsh realities of married life might actually be like. The woman who keeps her name, we suggest, may have a more realistic view of the gravity and difficulty of the step she is about to take. Loudly, to herself, her partner and the world, she is saying: I love you but I don't want to be absorbed into your identity. This seems to us a healthier and more sensible place from which to begin married life. When younger women have complained about the hassles of altering their names we have been unable to resist asking them why they bother. Almost invariably, we have been told 'I thought about it and it feels right'. Our fear is it symbolises a return to a notion of romance that – in the long run – rarely bodes well for the success of a marriage.

Marriage and identity

It's interesting to reflect that our reservations about our own marriages were based on a concern we would lose our identity even without a name change. In fact, quite the reverse has occurred – much to our surprise. Marriage actually increased our self-confidence, and perhaps that's also part of the reason our marriages have lasted so long. Marriage acted as a brake on too much emphasis on one part of our lives at the expense of another. We have both valued the wonderful career and life support and advice our husbands give us (hopefully they can say the same thing of us). It gave us perspective. They never wanted us to quit or stay home and iron their shirts, but then again, we probably wouldn't have married them if they had. We have made career moves that we wouldn't have been able to if either of us were a sole breadwinner. The financial implications for both partners of marriage and de facto relationships are significant, particularly today when both partners contribute to the kitty. We believe it is self-evident that the stability of your personal life must have a profound effect on your professional life and vice versa.

Yet we've often observed successful women in business advising younger women to keep their private life separate from their business life: to compartmentalise themselves, much as men have commonly done. This is not advice that we would give younger women – or men, for that matter – who are trying to forge a successful and interesting professional and personal life for themselves. Once you have decided to share your life with a partner your priorities change. Then children plunge your carefully constructed life into mayhem and it's difficult and probably stupid to pretend otherwise.

We have found it impossible to be one sort of person at work and another at home. No doubt this insistence on being employed as a whole person has had an adverse effect on our ability to reach the top of the corporate tree and can have the same effect on a man's career. But we fervently believe it has been absolutely central to our ability to create an interesting and (reasonably) balanced life. Once again, we believe this is why feminism has much to offer men, by relieving them of the unrelenting pressure to bring home as much bacon as they can. When both partners contribute, both partners have more options. It is true you cannot 'have it all', but this is not restricted to women's experience because *no one* has it all.

Sex

Feminism has also profoundly changed the relationship between modern women and sexual activity. Prior to feminism, women only had the right to say no to sex before they were married. Thanks to the legal concept of conjugal rights, after marriage, legally they could only say yes. Now they can say both yes and no to sex before marriage and yes and no to sex after marriage. This reflects a significant victory in their ability to control the integrity of their own bodies, and the importance of this cannot be overstated.

There's even academic research debunking the idea that

feminists are all unhappy lesbians with no sex life. 'Contrary to popular opinion, feminism and romance are not incompatible and feminism may actually improve the quality of heterosexual relationships,' according to Laurie Rudman and Julie Phelan, from Rutgers University in the US. They found that in heterosexual relationships, having a feminist partner was linked to a healthier and more mutually satisfying sex life. Men with feminist partners also reported both more stable relationships and greater sexual satisfaction. According to these results, feminism does not predict poor romantic relationships, in fact quite the opposite. Feminist women were more likely to be in a heterosexual romantic relationship than non-feminist women. ('Rutgers study says feminism can be good for heterosexual romance', TS-Si News Service, 18 October 2007)

The permission women now have to decide whether they actually feel like having sex, regardless of their marital status, has perhaps directly led to an increase in their ability to take pleasure in it. When your body is deemed to belong to someone else, it's bloody hard to respond with any kind of authentic pleasure. Given how dangerous the consequences of sexual intercourse were for women until the early 20th century, it's remarkable women ever had sex at all. Indeed, perhaps that's why they were not given much choice. There is a reason there are so many stepmothers in fairy tales; it is because so many women died in childbirth. Women have only had longer life spans than men for about a century or so.

The freedom to talk about female sexual pleasure (orgasm, clitoris, g-spots, masturbation, lesbianism and so on) without shame has been profoundly liberating, and is very recent. This candour has made many marriages and male/female relationships much more fulfilling and pleasurable than they used to be. Women often went into marriage ignorant of what was about to take place. Their terror in the marriage bed as a result can only be imagined, hardly a situation likely to lead to much mutual pleasure, unless the young husband was exceptionally sensitive and understanding. It wasn't just women who entered marriage in total ignorance. In her book *Parallel Lives* Phyllis Rose reveals that the famous Victorian philosopher John Ruskin was so appalled at his wife's pubic hair when he saw her naked on their wedding night that he considered her deformed and refused to consummate the relationship. Only a century ago, women who were told they should have no more children for medical reasons — often after horrendous labours — were given no information about how to avoid pregnancy. They had to rely on the consideration of a kind husband to avoid serious injury or even death.

Controlling our bodies

Women have always had to fight long and hard for even basic information about their own bodies. Dr Marie Stopes, one of the first women to qualify fully as a medical doctor in Britain at the turn of the previous century, spent years in an unconsummated marriage wondering why she could not get pregnant. When someone finally told her the reason, she was so alarmed about her ignorance, not just as a woman, but as a doctor, she began a lifelong campaign to ensure women received sex education and in particular contraceptive information, writing a famous book, *Married Love*. A book incidentally that was roundly and furiously criticised by religious leaders at the time.

When chloroform first began to be used to relieve the pain of childbirth, many moralists vigorously opposed it. They argued it was ordained by God that women suffer while giving birth as punishment for Eve's original sin. Fortunately for labouring women, the then head of the Church of England was often a labouring woman herself. Queen Victoria, who eventually gave birth nine times, grabbed chloroform, so to speak, with both hands, and made it acceptable. While she would never have claimed to be a feminist, this was in fact feminism in action. Who knows what might have happened had Victoria been a king. We would love ten dollars for every woman we know who has been told by her male obstetrician during childbirth to buck up or that the pain they are experiencing is really not too bad.

The consequences of this ignorance were bad enough for married women, but as always, for single women, it was catastrophic. Unmarried mothers, as we have pointed out, have always been punished for their sin. If they went ahead with their pregnancy, they were sent away from home, lies were told about illness or holidays, and their baby was whisked away from them as soon as it was born. One of the tragedies of the famous Australian author Charmian Clift's life was her continuous grief about the child she was forced to give up for adoption when she was in her teens. Clift's lost child was a secret she took with her to the grave and was only unearthed by the child herself, who as a grown woman searching for her birth parents discovered her mother had been Charmian. Tragically, by the time she found this out, Clift had already taken her own life.

Awful stories routinely appear in the media about the coercion exercised by doctors and nurses in past decades to persuade girls to give up their children. A relationship counsellor says that over a ten-year career, she has spent many hours working through the grief of women who gave up their children for adoption and the grief of children who were adopted out, but not one similar hour dealing with the emotional fall out from abortion. Not because she wasn't interested, but because her female clients who have had an abortion mention it in passing, and do not see it as a traumatic event. Single women who get pregnant have always been caught in a cleft stick. They're not supposed to have the baby, but they're not supposed to get rid of it either.

When two mothers abandoned babies in Sydney within weeks of each other in 2007 it unleashed a stunningly hysterical and hypocritical reaction. Whipped up by the popular media, there was speculation about what sort of women could abandon their babies and the unspeakable cruelty of their actions. We on the other hand thought the mothers, no doubt broke and possibly very young, had acted pragmatically. They had worked out they were on a hiding to nothing and would be struggling to support a child while attracting ill-disguised scorn from most corners of society (including the anti-abortion lobby no doubt) for even attempting to do so.

No one wants to have an abortion but, thanks to greater access to professional medical care, it is most often the unwanted pregnancy, not the ending of it, that is devastating. Like all adult human beings, women want to feel in control of their own fate and like all human beings they do not enjoy being controlled. It is a consequence of women's biology that to be fully autonomous they must also be trusted to control reproduction. The two are inextricably linked.

Most women have an abortion because they do not feel they can adequately parent the child they are carrying. Those who oppose their choice often sit in judgment about whether women even have the right to make such a decision. As feminism makes clear, it is the mother − primarily − who will do the unrelenting hard work for the 20 years it takes to raise a child well. So does anyone else really have any right to question her decision? You can't have it both ways − as we are often told by the neo-cons, it's all about mutual responsibility these days. (Not when it comes to parenting, apparently.) If we expect women to take the lion's share of the responsibility for raising well-adjusted kids, we must also give them the right to choose whether or not they are able to do so.

Society's expectations around women and fertility are so contradictory they are impossible for any woman to comply with. Even women who choose not to have children, or more often in our experience, who simply didn't meet a partner or have a chance to conceive, are often viciously attacked for their failure to live up to their 'biological destiny'. The ugly onslaught by Senator Bill Heffernan on the then Deputy Opposition Leader and now Deputy Prime Minister Julia Gillard over her lack of children appalled many Australians but also reflected some deeply held views about women and reproduction. Their failure to have children is likely to be seen as a character flaw, revealing a cold, selfish personality

– especially if they are successful. Some people choose not to have any children, as is their right, but for many their lack of children may be the source of great sorrow and regret.

In our own lives, we have directly benefited from the information, understanding and discussion that feminism has allowed us to have around sex, relationships and our bodies. This has allowed us to have more freedom and more control over our own destiny. But it's not just women who have gained, so have many men – not least the ones we sleep with. Thanks to feminism, they have been able to enjoy a much closer and more hands on relationship with their own children than any generation of men before them. Thanks to feminism, successful modern marriages are more like a partnership between equals than a relationship between servant and master. Many men are beginning to have more choices in their own lives, thanks to sharing the breadwinning responsibility with their wives. When a friend was asked how he had managed to do so well financially while choosing to limit his career to spend more time parenting, he simply replied: 'I married a feminist.'

However satisfying it may be for feminists like us to hear such a response, we are under no illusions that it is a common one, particularly from the husbands of the millions of women who live in a very different world.

10

Women of the world

It could all have been so different for us. Raised in middle class families in a stable liberal democracy during the 20th century we certainly did well in the lottery of birth. As women, we have been able to develop our potential and exercise choice over the kinds of life we would lead – who we'd marry, what kind of work we'd choose, how many children we would have – in ways that none of the women who have come before us have been able to do. Even in our own society, we are highly privileged women and we know it. Our gratitude for our remarkable good fortune – due in large part to modern feminism – is the motivation for writing this book. But we have tried not to take this for granted. Because we are interested in more than just the minutiae of our own lives, we have found it impossible to ignore the fate of many other not so fortunate women, in our own society and in others.

The tragic lives of women all over the world, reported in the news or books and articles we happen to be reading, have also formed much of the content of our ongoing conversations. It is not enough nor is it fair that women like us have pretty good lives, when others live and die in such anguish. We want all women to have the opportunities and rights we enjoy. However, our concern is not entirely altruistic. It is impossible to watch television reports of faceless women in blue burkhas begging among puddles, or being executed in the back of a truck and not feel something – outrage and compassion, certainly, but also a cold chill of fear. Watching a devout Muslim woman plead her case on TV recently, we were mesmerised by her appearance. She was so completely covered from head to toe – apart from a slit for her eyes – that she even wore leather gloves over her hands. Her image made Jane feel so claustrophobic she had to go outside and take some deep breaths. It is impossible for us to see such women and not feel that there but for the grace of God go I. As we watch the plight of many women in the world we can imagine what African-Americans must have felt watching the consequences of apartheid in South Africa.

What we see also makes us ask why. Why is it always women who must be so controlled and oppressed? What is so uniquely terrifying about the female human form that it must be comprehensively erased and punished? This chapter is a record of the many conversations we've had where we tried to explore these questions and come up with a few possible answers. We know that by writing it we may be accused of taking a narrow, culturally imperialist view, but we're prepared to take that risk. Our moral code is a simple one. If we wouldn't like to be treated in this way we suspect other women no matter where and how they live probably don't enjoy this treatment either. We write about these issues because we have been so lucky, and because we feel for women whose lives are so difficult and constrained. But also because we remain aware that the gains Western women have made are not immutable and – without eternal vigilance – may not last.

We feel a particular urgency about this topic because of what is often referred to as the clash of civilisations – between the secular, industrialised West and the growing religious fundamentalism of much of the developing world. We cannot help feeling much of this clash is about the relative status and freedom of women. It seems to us, therefore, that this is a topic feminism needs to address.

Controlling women

Religious authoritarians and fundamentalists, it seems, have always been obsessively concerned with controlling sexuality, particularly female sexuality, and it is hard to think of a religion that has not sought to exert power and make rules about how women live and breed. It is not a coincidence that almost no modern religions empower women as priests – with the honourable exceptions of the Episcopalian and Uniting Churches in the US and Australia respectively. Religions of all kinds often seem to fear women and respond to this emotional confusion by both demonising and idealising them.

For example, in the Christian tradition, there is the perennial madonna/whore dichotomy. In this view of the world, good women (madonnas) do what men tell them, and bad women (whores) do what they want. Christianity, traditionally, even goes so far as to put the blame for humankind's supposed original state of sin squarely on the shoulders of the female – a powerful psychological weapon if ever there was one. These traditions are of course thousands of years old and both they and their female adherents have come a long way since then. Liberal denominations and theologians, it must be said, in all kinds of churches and religions have often fundamentally changed their view of the role of women. Nevertheless, it is surprising how, particularly in more conservative and orthodox religious circles, old habits die hard.

At a humanist seminar on the separation of Church and State in Melbourne in 2006 a panel of religious liberals were challenged on their respective religious traditions' treatment of women. Not one even attempted to argue that their church had a proud record. Indeed, the woman representing the Anglican Church confessed that it broke her heart to hear and see the way many of the leaders of her church treated and spoke about women, particularly about their ordination.

Women and authoritarianism

Religions, by and large, whether you are talking tribal animism, the ancient Aztecs or Catholicism, exercise much of their energy around human birth and death. Once, they were the unchallenged final arbiters, now secular scientists and doctors (most of whom are male, but some of whom are female) have taken over much of that territory. Arguments about pragmatism versus ethics continually burn hot between the scientists and the clergy. And the issue that flames particularly high remains abortion. After all, allowing women the right to choose whether or not they will carry a pregnancy to full term is one of the few single issues that gives them control of both life and death.

Abortion is not just a religious issue of course. As the book *Freakonomics* (Steven D. Levitt & Stephen J. Dubner 2005) points out, the communist Ceauçescu regime in Romania enacted draconian anti-abortion, anti-contraception and pro-birth policies at the end of the last century, where women of childbearing age who had not become pregnant were interrogated and forcibly medically examined by agents of the state to coerce them into reproducing. The horrifying images that emerged after the fall of Ceauçescu of starved and neglected unwanted children rocking themselves obsessively in Romanian orphanages depicted the direct result of such extreme authoritarian control over women's bodies and rights. At the other end of the spectrum, the policies instituted by the authoritarian communist regime in China in pursuit of its one child policy have also resulted in horrors: forced late-term abortions for some Chinese women, the preponderance of abandoned female children, also filmed rocking themselves obsessively in bleak orphanages, and female infanticide.

The tragic spread of AIDS in Africa has been the result of many factors, including traditional tribal practices and beliefs about the curative properties of virginity. But it is troubling, particularly given the strong social justice agenda and efforts of the Catholic Church in many parts of the developing world, to learn of the misinformation the Church has spread about the permeability of condoms. This has undoubtedly reduced the effectiveness of the fight against AIDS in that continent, and, many argue, has therefore helped to spread the infection and so caused the eventual early death of untold numbers of Africans. To take just one example; four out of ten girls are estimated to be HIV-positive in Kenya, the highest infection rate in the world

('Sex and the Holy City', *Panorama*, BBC, 12 October 2003).

In stark contrast, Australia has led the world in stopping the spread of AIDS. As the documentary ('Rampant: How a City Stopped a Plague' ABC, 3 December 2007) points out, this was achieved thanks to a pragmatic, harm-minimisation strategy led by secular scientists such as the then Health Minister Dr Neal Blewett. Against the protests of the moralists, they adopted a needle exchange program to stop the infection spreading into the intravenous drug-using population, and enlisted the support and active participation of the gay and lesbian community and sex workers. Condom use became the norm in these communities and refusal to adopt safe sex practices, even in the sex industry, became simply unacceptable.

As a result thousands of lives were saved and Australia is now cited as an example of world's best practice in the control of AIDS. Given the greater susceptibility of women to be infected with the virus during sexual intercourse – as illustrated by the ghastly outlook for the girls of Kenya – there is absolutely no doubt that many of the lives saved were female. Interestingly, when the newly discovered cervical cancer vaccine was developed to prevent young women being infected by the genital warts virus, which can lead to cancer, there was some criticism about the immunisation program from moralists. The essence of their concern appeared to be that such protection would encourage promiscuity amongst young women! Apparently they still believe the wages of sin should be death.

It is hard to escape the conclusion sometimes that those aggressively stating a pro-life stance only apply it to the lives of the unborn. The living are apparently more easily ignored, or so the rhetoric implies, particularly if saving them might undermine some authoritarian and extraordinarily out of touch and ignorant beliefs about the reality of the lives of women and girls. In many developing societies, for example, regardless of the moralists' teachings on the subject, it is virtually impossible for women to refuse sex, particularly inside marriage. Given that conjugal rights were only legally abolished a few decades ago in our own society, it is hardly surprising that women in the third world are still battling for such basic human rights.

Indeed, there is something chillingly familiar about the attitude to women revealed by the conversation Pope John Paul II had with Dr Nafis Sadik, the Director of the UN Population Fund from 1987–2000. As she related it, the pontiff revealed a frightening view of male and female relationships.

> I was telling him ... many women became pregnant not because they wanted to but because their ... you know ... spouses imposed themselves on them. He said: 'Don't you think that the irresponsible behaviour of men is caused by women?' ('Sex and The Holy City', *Panorama*, BBC, 12 October 2003)

Woman as temptress

To us, these remarks are reminiscent of the attitude revealed by the former-Governor General Archbishop Peter Hollingworth (ex-Anglican Archbishop of Brisbane) in his defence of the priest accused of seducing one of his female students, aged 14, on the ABC's *Australian Story*. 'My information is that it was rather the other way around,' he said of the seduction. This attitude to the duty of care owed by an adult priest and teacher towards a 14-year-old student boggles the mind. Consider for a moment what Archbishop Hollingworth's response might have been if the student in question had been a boy. It is inconceivable that he would have attempted the same defence.

According to many religious frameworks if women are temptresses they are then to blame for whatever men do to them. At some level, conscious or otherwise, religious authoritarians seem to burden women with most of the guilt and blame for sexual assault and even for reproducing. And in our own culture, while this attitude may have gone underground in more recent times thanks to feminism, it is not so long ago that it was manifest. An older friend of ours remembers giving birth to her first child in a Catholic hospital as a frightened but married 20 year old. As she moaned with the pain and effort, a midwife nun came and stood grim-faced at the door. 'Well,' she said to our friend, 'You made your bed, now you lie in it.' But it wasn't just the religious who lacked any sympathy for birthing women. The mother of a friend gave birth in a secular, public hospital in the 1950s and as she grunted with the pain had her face slapped by the matron.

The demonisation of women as vessels of potential corruption and temptation is a pillar of many religious traditions. This came to a head in 2006 during the trial of a family of Muslim brothers accused of the brutal rape in Sydney of some young non-Muslim girls. One of the accused used his religious belief and its view of acceptable behaviour by women as part of his defence. Predictably this caused a storm of controversy at the time including these comments by a Muslim cleric Sheik Hilali:

> If you take out uncovered meat and place it outside on the street, or in the garden or in the park, or in the backyard without a cover, and the cats come and eat it ... whose fault is it, the cats' or the uncovered meat? The uncovered meat is the problem.

The sheik then said: 'If she was in her room, in her home, in her hijab, no problem would have occurred.' He said women were 'weapons' used by 'Satan' to control men. 'It is said in the state of zina (adultery), the responsibility falls 90 per cent of the time on the woman. Why? Because she possesses the weapon of enticement (igraa)' ('Muslim leader blames women for sex attacks', Richard Kerbaj, *The Australian,* 26 October 2006).

But attitudes like this don't require a dramatic rape to be brought into the open. A year earlier, in 2005, we heard much the same from another Muslim cleric, as reported in *The Age*:

> 'Every minute in the world a woman is raped, and she has no one to blame but herself, for she has displayed her beauty to the whole world,' Sheikh Feiz Muhammad told a packed public meeting in the Bankstown Town Hall last month. 'Strapless, backless, sleeveless – they are nothing but satanical. Mini-skirts, tight jeans – all this to tease men and to appeal to (their) carnal nature. 'There was pressure on Muslim women to unveil,' the

sheikh said, and this was because 'they want you to be available for their gross, disgusting, filthy abomination! They want you to be a sex symbol!' The woman who wore the hijab was hiding her beauty from the eyes of 'lustful, hungry wolves', he said. ('Religious extremists an insult to our values', Pamela Bone, *The Age*, 14 April 2005)

Women are, once again, held responsible for male sexual behaviour, and to blame if such behaviour is exposed. This attitude is not confined to formal religion, but reveals itself in all sorts of traditional and tribal cultures. The recent prosecutions of many Pitcairn islanders (descendants of the Bounty mutineers) for endemic child sexual abuse are another example of this. It was the women who made the complaints who were demonised on Pitcairn, rather than those they accused. Australian author Colleen McCullough who is married to a Bounty descendant rationalised the abuse by saying 'It's Polynesian to break your girls in at 12' ('Author backs sex islanders', *Edinburgh Evening News*, 16 November 2004). Even the language used by McCullough is revealing; who wants to be 'broken in' after all?

Perhaps in each of these examples as Simone de Beauvoir suggested in *The Second Sex* men are projecting their own unacceptable feelings and emotions onto 'the other'; thus women are held responsible for the behaviour and reactions of some men. Sheikh Feiz Muhammad's controversial comments, for example, blame a woman's appearance for making a man rape her. There's a breathtaking lack of logic here. Does the Sheikh believe the rich make poorer men steal just by being rich, and that this an acceptable defence? Of course he doesn't, and nor does his (or any other) religion. In Islam, according to Sharia law, it is acceptable to cut off the hand of a thief, no matter how flagrantly the person who has been robbed was flaunting their wealth.

It has become commonplace to see fundamentalist Christian preachers fall spectacularly from grace when some sexual peccadillo of their own is brought to light, to the point that whenever we hear someone fulminating about sex and morality, we now automatically suspect them of being in denial about kinky sexual behaviour. Naughty of us, we know, but – just like the men who cannot help but respond to the incitement of Western dress – we can't help ourselves. Feminism is helping women recognise this process: the unfairness of this blame and the moral guardianship it imposes on women.

The clash of civilisations

While it is currently fashionable to trivialise or ignore the importance of the change in the role and status of women in the West – hence feminism becoming the F word – there are many in the world who see very clearly just how important and revolutionary this has been. Often these are people who do not like the changes and sense that they indicate a deep and terrifying threat to the established order.

> The contents of religions are determined by social
> relationships ... the battle for Islam is a worldwide
> battle for the preservation of male power. Muslim men
> are confronted in the West (and by globalisation) with

totally different relations between the sexes, while their
self-respect is traditionally based on their masculine
'honour'. A man's 'honour' depends on the behaviour
of his wives, daughters and sisters, and he therefore
sees it as a right and a necessity that he can impose
his will on these women. Masculine honour implies the
idea of male superiority as well as the concrete power
of men over women. Both have diminished considerably
in the Western world. Muslim fundamentalism is gender
fundamentalism. ('Shoot the Women First', Part 3,
Jolande Withuis, <newmatilda.com>, 5 November 2007)

Some of Withuis' views have been echoed by local commentator
Paul Sheehan. If these writers are correct, the war of the sexes
may have become an actual war. George Bush and other Western
leaders may prefer to articulate this as a fight for Christian values,
democracy or 'our way of life', but it may really be a bloody battle
over the position of women. The appalling treatment of women
under the Taliban in Afghanistan brought this into stark relief.

In a small way, Jane noticed this clash some time ago through
her work on global advertising accounts. Advertising's rapid
globalisation in the 1990s sent warnings about this growing
tension long before many saw it coming. This globalisation has
been unproblematic when it comes to messages about products
aimed at men — cars, travel, electronic goods and the like — but
advertisers pretty quickly came up against severe barriers when
they tried to create global advertising aimed at women, particularly
in the areas of personal care such as cosmetics, shampoos and bath
products. They tripped over strong taboos in Islamic cultures about

how women could be presented and talked about. Indeed, during the advertising campaign for the Commonwealth games held in Malaysia, something very important went completely unnoticed. Amongst all the usual images of aspiring athletes there were few images of sportswomen. In Muslim Malaysia such images were unacceptable.

The conscious liberation of the female race

According to Jolande Withuis 'the ideal Muslim woman is a mother who bears many sons.' Scarily, it's not so long ago that this was the ideal Christian woman, too.

> The lowest of the low in a Muslim country are divorced women, followed closely by the almost equally despised unwed women. It is clear that the traditional role model does not offer the life these girls want, but they are also not able to get away from the obligation or the pressure to be feminine as defined by their culture, environment or faith. They do not want to be looked down on as women. They accept the imposed division of mankind into two unequal, totally different types, but they still want another kind of life than the one traditionally allotted to their gender. They display modern and self-conscious behaviour, and feel the desire to be of significance in a religious community that has always been the domain of men. Cloaked in all-covering clothing, they roam the Internet looking for texts that give women the right to join the jihad.' (Withuis 2007)

Withuis examines the consequences when women do become radical Muslims. According to her, their determination to prove that while they may have the body of a weak woman they have the soul of a fierce warrior means they often become even more extreme in their violence than their male counterparts. Using examples that range from female Christian martyrs of the Middle Ages to the modern anorexic, Withuis argues that sexist norms give many women – particularly those with energy and talent – little way out other than through extreme behaviour.

When we first read these articles we were chilled by their familiarity. All of these restrictions on what women may or may not do have echoes in Western history, and the illustrations she used of martyred saints and anorexic obsessives from European society and tradition remind us that these are not problems exclusive to Muslim women. Feminism has given us a rational alternative to such extreme reactions and it is heartening to see that it is having an effect in many Muslim countries too. There are many brave and indomitable Muslim women fighting for the human rights of women in their own societies: women who battle honour killings and acid defacements of women in Pakistan and who defended widows in India; the extraordinary courage and commitment of the women of RAWA (Revolutionary Afghan Women's Army) in their fight against the Taliban; and individuals like Ayaan Hirsi Ali, Dutch-Somalian author and filmmaker and Malalai Joya, outspoken 29-year-old Afghani MP, who daily face the threat of persecution and death in their fight for the human rights of women in Islamic societies. These women are remarkable and we are awed by them.

Their struggles have made us wonder if the battle for women's freedom isn't possibly the hardest fight in history. After all, when black people fight for their rights, they do so against white people, when Palestinians fight for their homeland, they do so against Israelis, Hutus murder Tutsis, Muslims fight Christians, Buddhist monks battle Mianmar military. But when women fight for their rights they must battle their fathers, their brothers, their husbands and hardest of all, their sons. Perhaps this is why so many women throughout the centuries have shied away from claiming their own rights, or have run out of heart so quickly. It is bitter indeed to have as oppressors the very people who are meant to love us.

Hard though the battle may be, particularly for women who are trying to survive in some of the poorest and most unstable countries on earth, it remains vitally important – and not just because it benefits women. Indeed there is now growing evidence that improvement in education and opportunities for women is the best way to improve life for every member of a society.

Poverty and feminism

To the authoritarian traditionalists, feminism appears to be nothing but a bad thing, even, perhaps, evil. To ordinary people however, struggling to live a decent and reasonable life and hopefully create a better one for their children, the opportunities that feminism represents, if not the idea itself, is a lifeline. Lord David Puttnam, head of the British arm of UNICEF, says that when he is asked by philanthropists how they can get the most bang for their donated buck, he always says they should donate it to women and girls because that is the way to raise living standards for the whole society.

Micro credit and micro loans are usually loans of extremely small sums of money, hundreds of dollars at most. These loans are often extended exclusively to women in the developing world and enable them to buy a treadle sewing machine or the tools needed to set up a cottage industry. The idea of such micro credit for the poorest women in the world was greeted with derision by the mainstream banks when they were launched in the 1970s, but this response very quickly turned to admiration. Such has been their success they are now an established tool in international lending. The UN made 2005 the National Year of Microcredit. The loans have an extremely low default rate and the women proved that with only the smallest amounts of capital they could set up profitable businesses that both increased their own autonomy and vastly improved the outcomes for their family as a whole. Such loans are credited with lifting the living standards of entire communities.

Other studies have revealed that in countries where there is less physical mistreatment of women, men are also less likely to be murdered or the victims of violence. It is no coincidence that the countries with the highest standards of living are also those with the most egalitarian attitudes towards women and their opportunities. The two things, many are now beginning to understand, are directly related. Hold women back and you retard the whole society.

So why do so many human societies continue to block the progress of women so tenaciously?

Passing on your DNA

As we've puzzled over the tragedy of so many women's lives, we've used our understanding of feminism to try and come to grips with why so many women are condemned to poverty, illiteracy and abuse. This has led to us right back to biological determinism. We're not claiming to have found 'the answer', but here is our take on what is going on.

Once it was believed the control of women was necessary because women were intrinsically weaker and less capable than men and so needed their protection. Thanks to feminism and technology which has largely negated the physical power difference between the sexes – a woman can shoot a gun just as fatally as any man – that view has started to disappear, at least in the West. So if women are not naturally inferior to men, then why is there still such a universal need to control them?

Perhaps the answers lie in our biology. We have been fascinated with much of the research and discussion around the subject. The knowledge that one has passed on one's DNA is problematic for males. Not just human males, either. Throughout the animal kingdom males fight, sometimes to the death, for the right to mate and pass on their genes. In primates, if a previously dominant male is defeated and chased off, the young of the group, his genetic offspring, are at great risk from the new leader. Indeed, a recent report ('Intrasexual selection and testis size in strepsirhine primates,' Peter M Kappeler, *Behavioural Ecology*, Vol 8 No 1) links the size of a primate's testicles to the relative promiscuity of the female of the species. Male chimpanzees have huge testicles and female chimpanzees are very free with their favours. Gorillas have tiny testicles and tightly-controlled harems. Human testicles are somewhere in between. The size of testicles and amount of sperm produced is nature's way of giving the male its best chance of passing on his genes.

This problem simply does not exist for female animals. A woman who gives birth knows she has succeeded in bequeathing 50 per cent of her genetic material to the future. She has fulfilled her biological task. A man, on the other hand, cannot be so sure. DNA testing in recent years has in fact confirmed what many suspected: that some men have been unwittingly putting their energy and resources into children who are not their own. These revelations have been considered of such importance they have made headlines around the world. Unsurprising when you consider that the investment now required to raise a child has increased exponentially. The number of marriages that break down has also exploded, and men are perhaps warier than ever before of accepting both the responsibility and the insecurity that inevitably accompanies fatherhood. An insecurity that over millennia has led to traditions like displaying bloodied bed sheets after the consummation of a marriage, female circumcision, foot binding, burkhas, chastity belts, eunuchs guarding harems, honour killings and one thousand and one other devices designed to keep a woman from conceiving another man's child.

Looked at from a purely biological perspective, it is no wonder society agrees with nature. Men who spread their seed far and wide are if not celebrated at least tolerated, because it maximises their chance of passing on their genes. A woman who is promiscuous however is terrifying. Who knows which man's child she could end up foisting on her partner? Society attempts to control such women using overt disapproval, insults, religion and of course the law.

Given all of this, it's little wonder that feminism has become a dirty word. It upsets something fundamental and breaks some of the most basic and universal taboos. This is why it is frightening, why its progress is often slow, but also why it is so important. Indeed, in the next chapter, we argue that one of the ways society is currently attempting to control women is by denigrating the very name of the movement that has brought us so far.

11

Why feminism is the F word

The awareness of the plight of women that feminism brings and the progress the movement has made over the centuries is probably the only hope for improving women's lives all over the globe. It is a feminist perspective that keeps women like us alert to the fate of women in other countries. We do not accept a culturally relativist explanation for the continued oppression of women in other parts of the world. Nor do we accept that because they are so much worse off than Australian women, we have no right to fight against systemic prejudice and injustice in our own society. This is however one of the many ways feminism is undermined and dismissed.

Women like us run the risk of being accused of at best cultural insensitivity and at worst overt racism if we object to the way women in developing countries are the victims of discrimination. Indeed, many women in the developing world struggle to cope with more children than they want or can afford due, we believe, to a lack of feminism. Meanwhile many women in developed economies like Australia struggle with just the opposite, a situation which is blamed on the F word.

'Our generation is part of a failed experiment,' said a smartly dressed woman in her thirties, with a senior job in a large company who approached us after a business seminar. She said that at her age, she would like to be married and having children but there was little chance of that, given the hours she worked and the demands of her job. Most of her friends, she said, felt the same way.

Women, exhausted from working the double shift, are used as evidence by critics who claim the natural order of gender roles will out. Women should be at home and can't cut it in the wider world, they crow, and feminism is to blame for giving them silly ideas. Meanwhile, women like us sit on the sidelines throwing the occasional Molotov cocktail into the fray and trying to point out that for many women it is the unreasonable demands they bear and lack of support in the workplace and at home which leaves them exhausted and disillusioned. And some of them, who feel they have missed their chance to have children, are left grief stricken. How did our generation, with everything we had going for us, come to this?

The timing that sees job demands peak at the same point as the loud ticking of the body clock doesn't justify labelling feminism a failed experiment, in our opinion. Surely the alternative of a few decades ago – housework and kids – was not the bee's knees either. Our young friend ignored the fact that just 30 years ago the professional firm she worked for would not have let her through the door, much less promoted her. But this success has also delivered one of feminism's biggest challenges: how feminism itself has become a dirty word. To find out how this happened we need to revisit some of the major themes of our earlier chapters.

I'm not a feminist but ...

Unsurprisingly, women such as our 'failed experiment' friend often seem allergic to the very word feminism, which symbolises their discontent. This is the same age group we frequently address at seminars and conferences who repudiate the word, yet can't believe that just four decades ago women had to resign from the public service when they got married, or that up until the early 1970s they couldn't get a home loan without a male guarantor. But many of them worryingly assume these hard fought battles are well and truly won and the debate has moved on. Or that feminism is stuck in a 1960s time warp and holds no relevance for them.

Are well-educated young women rejecting feminism? Yes and no, says lawyer, mother and board member of law firm Freehills, Rebecca Davies. With a critical group of younger women lawyers in the firm now in their childbearing years, Davies is trying hard to get them to stay and make the firm change to help that process. Philosophically feminism is a dirty word to many of these young women she told us, and it's reflected in the number changing their names when they get married. What's more, she reckons many are getting married younger than in her generation. But, interestingly, they are not resistant to the idea of having women's networks, and taking advantage of what those networks do.

Part of the Freehill's support system for women includes coaching by sociolinguist Margaret Byrne from United Group

Consulting. Byrne's PhD research explored how men and women behave in meetings, and the impact that differing behaviour has on their chance of landing an executive role. Her interest in what is happening with the Gen X and Y cohort is not merely theoretical; she has two daughters in this age group. In the early 1970s, many women believed things would be radically different for their daughters. Lots of women were at home with small babies going out of their minds; depression was widespread as they saw their opportunities slipping away. But it's more complicated for her daughters than for her. Byrne told us:

> These days each choice has an implication. And it
> does make it more challenging ... and more exciting. I
> do think that the issues facing young women are more
> complicated. It's an apolitical generation. Issues are more
> subtle and nuanced. Not straight sexism – when you talk
> to young women lawyers, for instance, about sexism it's
> often difficult for them to name it because it's covert
> and subtle. That makes tackling it head-on quite difficult.
> It's become embedded in the culture.

Of course not all young women reject the politics around women and their place in the world. Well-known *Sydney Morning Herald* columnist Annabel Crabb puts it this way:

> The more I think about it, the more I think the daggy
> old name for the women's movement, Women's
> Liberation, is the best possible summary for how I feel
> about feminism as a 35 year old, having now identified

myself as a feminist for nearly 20 years. I think when I
first started being interested in feminism I was interested
in the structure of the political discipline – the formal
thought, the history and the political theory of it.
Needless to say, this is while I was an undergraduate at
university. Feminism, at that time, gave me an extremely
confident and well-referenced view about how I thought
the world worked. Of course, you develop a far more
qualified view when you move out of university and into
the workplace and into the world ... Back then, I think I
saw feminism as a major issue in my thoughts and life
– now I see it as a framework more than anything else.

This generation certainly sees its opportunities as unlimited, until
they reach childbearing age, and want to have the job and the
lifestyle and the family. According to US writer Deborah Siegel
many women born from about 1980 don't think there is any
need to be part of a movement because the hurdles have all been
successfully negotiated.

The trendy notion that we are living in a 'post-feminist'
era has lulled many young women into inertia. Young
women assume their equality and take it for granted, but
they aren't the first to dismiss the movement prematurely.
The word 'postfeminist' was first uttered in 1919 – just
a few decades after the coining of the word feminist.
(Deborah Siegel, *Sisterhood Interrupted*, 2007, p.7)

The idea we have somehow fought and won the battle for gender equity is woefully premature, Siegel adds. And rejecting the F word means this group tends to ignore the strength of collective action, which characterised the women's movement. Only by banding together could women manage to galvanise public opinion and win women the right to vote, as the distinguished Australian historian, feminist and author Jill Ker Conway pointed out in an interview with Catherine in 2006. In the US, and even internationally, women formed networks that lobbied hard for women's suffrage and had great success, she explained, but there is a very different attitude and organisation of social activism in an era of rampant individualism.

Social cohesion helped make some major inroads for Australian women's rights but progress has stalled, according to one of our best-known feminists, Anne Summers. Her 2003 book *The End of Equality* made the point that a backsliding was possible without further concerted effort by women acting together. And Australian social researcher Hugh Mackay has also found young women to be highly dismissive of the feminism they associate with the previous generation or so.

'Ask any woman under the age of 30 and she's likely to tell you she isn't a feminist', (Mackay, 2007, p. 27). This bunch generally believe feminists got it wrong, he writes, and were too prescriptive about jobs and housework. Now it's OK to be liberated and do whatever you want, wear what you like and laugh at sexist jokes if you feel like it. They have seen the problems their mothers encountered in trying to balance a number of burdens and don't want a bar of it. And older feminists are outraged and appalled that younger women don't get it.

Annabel Crabb talks about generational conflict this way:

I know there are tensions now among older feminists about the way young women esteem their feminist forebears, or utilise the freedom that was won for them. But freedom is freedom isn't it? It's not just a word on a banner. If feminism is serious about freedom, it can't really justify sneering at Britney Spears or whatever, in my opinion. I mean, sneer at Britney Spears as a matter of taste; it would be derelict not to. But as a matter of politics? I don't think so.

We certainly worry that younger women take some of their rights for granted without understanding they can be eroded. But as middle-aged feminists we too believe in the principles Mackay says younger women adhere to – having the right to live in different ways without following a set of rules. We see this as entirely congruent with our understanding of feminist principles. In fact, we believe the feminism these younger women are rejecting is one that was constructed – not by feminists – but by those who opposed them. We appreciate that liberty for women is built on some hard won battles of an earlier era of feminist activism, and did not logically evolve. It's also worrying to hear many young women – as we often do – tell us they already have a viable suite of options as they pursue careers and become mothers. They believe, as we will see, that their decisions are theirs alone and they have genuine agency – the ability to make choices and to impose them on the world. But unfortunately it usually isn't that straightforward.

The false dichotomy

The early feminist movement concentrated on winning basic legal rights for women, but by the time second-wave feminism became active around the 1960s the famous call to action was all about getting women out of the house and into the workplace. The notion of equality with men on the job became the primary focus. In the process, house and family work was by default seen as a poor option for enlightened females. It was to prove a costly delineation. The women's movement split into camps: and the seeds of today's backlash may have been inadvertently sown. Even as feminism helped prise open the doors to universities and workplaces, it became synonymous with the denigration of all family work.

> In the popular imagination, feminism came to be associated with careerists whose model of equality married them to money rather than to caregiving ... Although it made perfect sense for Friedan to argue in 1962 that women should join the workforce without waiting for changes from their husbands, their employers, or the government, it quickly became apparent that 'having it all' under those circumstances often leads to exhausted women doing it all. (Williams 2000, p.47)

It's easy to forget, from our privileged vantage point in the 21st century, how a few decades have made an incredible difference to the lives of many women. In their haste to raise the consciousness of scores of housewives those postwar feminists achieved much.

But perhaps like us they could not have predicted the barriers to reorganising domestic work and childcare. Housework was seen as the enemy and a handicap in that earlier era, and it still is for many women, but somehow the role of mother and carer was often tarred with the same brush, or its emotional pull ignored altogether.

As women scurried off to study or to the office or factory the optimists imagined a well-ordered childcare system would develop to pick up the slack, and most women would welcome this arrangement. It was a scenario that certainly didn't materialise but also failed to take into account the emotional impact for women of this massive shift, even those tantalised by the thought of a life beyond suburbia.

It was fair enough for feminists to complain about patriarchy and male suppression but pragmatic women twigged that men would have to come on board for the ride at some stage or there was little chance of permanent change. As we've examined, power and status are not easily surrendered and a lot of men quickly recognised the invasion of their turf, and the potential for something they didn't like the sound of one little bit: no dinner on the table and picking up their own dirty socks. As the backlash gathered momentum it gave birth to an enduring cliché. Now feminists were all branded radical, bra-burning weirdos who hated men as well as housewives and mothers. Sadly the warped version not only resonated but the feminists' legacy of revolutionary change for the better got lost in the melee.

The clichés didn't disappear, and still do the rounds today. The F word now has the capacity to send many women into automatic denial. It's OK to talk about women's rights if the language and ideas are not too extreme. Corporates tend to use the word 'diversity' as a euphemism and spout platitudes about their commitment to action. The market economy, of course, needs women's paid and unpaid labour to keep those wheels of commerce turning so lip service is paid to a 'work/life balance' agenda in many businesses. But just as second-wave feminists are accused of ignoring the domestic side of labour, so employers have also paid little attention to the enormous issue of who does the work at home.

Backlash rhetoric

It's not just women born since 1980 who spurn feminism. Many women of our age are confused about what the term means and uneasy about its connotations. We've asked a range of women of all age groups about feminism and found some true believers but many who think it is just old-fashioned polemic with little relevance to their lives.

'Do you mean like Germaine Greer?' said a 45-year-old woman in astonishment when we asked her if she was a feminist. Several other women simply said they weren't feminists because they didn't like the label. 'I just don't know what it means any more,' said another. Some believed feminism was prescriptive and dour – a system of belief that leaves no room for fun or self-expression. (How Betty Friedan, Gloria Steinem and Germaine Greer would hate that idea). Others had absorbed the clichés about left wing radicals and anti-male harridans and felt repelled.

In the business world, Catherine has found a small but influential group of women in senior jobs believe feminism equates to a victim mentality from those who want a fast track to success without doing the hard yards. Interestingly this view is often expressed by women who have made it to the top and 'pulled the ladder up after them'. Because they firmly believe there are no impediments for women (as long as they behave like men) these executives oppose any special measures to attract and retain women. 'If I had to do it the hard way then so should everyone,' they seem to think. In the world of advertising, Jane has lost count of the number of times she was 'kindly' advised to stop calling herself a feminist because it was holding back her career. In fact, her refusal to take this advice led to numerous opportunities to build a public and media profile. It must also be said, however, that while it opened some unexpected doors, it also slammed shut, locked and bolted quite a few more traditional ones.

There's also been a litany of anti-feminist rhetoric in the media over recent years. From references to 'Germaine Greer and that sad old dishrag we used to call feminism' ('Please pretty lady won't you take my seat', Janice Breen Burns, *The Age*, 17 November 2007) to comments by celebrities such as former Spice Girl Geri Halliwell (remember girl power?): 'It's about labelling. For me feminism is about bra burning lesbianism. It's very unglamorous' (*Guardian*, 25 October 2007). What passes for glamour these days is a topic we'll come to a little later, but Halliwell's opinion is a popular one.

We were also astonished and bemused to read that comedy character Ja'mie from the hit ABC TV program 'Summer Heights High' was apparently a by-product of feminism, according to Monash sociology academic Jennifer Sinclair ('It's all about me: Summer Heights High's Ja'mie is feminism's worst nightmare',

The Age, 25 October 2007). This appallingly selfish and venal teenage character was 'an unintended consequence of feminism.'

> Feminism has challenged the idea that women should be quiet, docile and nice. On that score, Ja'mie could be feminism's poster girl. The gung-ho 'you go girl' kind of feminism that swells the chests of principals of private girls schools when their students outgun the boys at whatever endeavour is on the go is just what the feminist doctor ordered. The idea that girls should ever take a moment to consider other people in their quest to be and do whatever they want is simply not on the radar.

Goodness, we thought, that particular element of feminism must have passed us by. We believed it was about independence and access to opportunity but can't recall feminism teaching us to achieve through kneecapping nastiness. To the contrary, a philosophy with fairness and equal rights at its heart always conveyed the opposite notion to us – that all people, regardless of gender, should be able to treat each other with respect.

Sure, Sinclair maintained that Ja'mie was an 'unintended' consequence of feminism but it seems to us that drawing such conclusions is an intended result of a highly effective smear campaign that equates niceness with traditional roles and nastiness with self-determination. One cancels out the other, according to this interpretation, and that's an all-too-familiar theme echoed in the pervasive 'mummy wars'. It pops up whenever feminism is blamed for social ills. All the bloody time, in other words.

Feminism has even been blamed for brainwashing intelligent women to such an extent they failed to have a family. This was the premise in television journalist Virginia Haussegger's *Wonder Woman* (2005) where she blamed older feminists for encouraging her to have a career and postpone childbearing until it was too late. You see, for women who never quite grow up, it's always Mum's fault. And these days, if the publicity is to be believed, feminism is apparently encouraging young women to behave like porn stars.

Raunch

It's been convenient to blame feminism for so many social ills that it now bears the burden of some completely contradictory trends. The rise of raunch culture is a case in point. A couple of years ago Catherine interviewed high profile *New York Times* and *Washington Post* columnist Maureen Dowd. As the conversation turned to young women and the rise of raunch, she looked increasingly puzzled. She couldn't work it out. Why were young women turning to porn images as style icons, and willingly stripping off in bars, or pole dancing while often, most astoundingly, attributing this trend to feminism? What on earth was going on?

Dowd is an acute observer of what happens when women upset the established order. But she finds it hard to work out why these young women with such opportunities believe raunchiness liberates them. Perhaps, she mused, it was a compensation for outdoing the boys in academic work and an attempt to re-establish their 'feminine' credentials.

It puzzles us too. Perhaps it's another example of an

'unintended consequence' of a certain interpretation of feminism. Pandering to male sexual fantasies doesn't appear liberating to us – nor much fun. As journalist Ariel Levy pointed out in her book *Female Chauvinist Pigs*, materialism and today's consumption culture have aided and abetted the process which she said could be dubbed the 'Paris Hilton effect'. 'The proposition that having the most simplistic, plastic stereotypes of female sexuality constantly reiterated throughout our culture somehow proves that we are sexually liberated and personally empowered has been offered to us and we have accepted it,' she writes. 'But we know this just doesn't make any sense' (Levy 2005, p. 197).

When Catherine interviewed her in 2005, Levy linked the rise of raunch to the backlash against women's progress. Levy was concerned that the whole feminist movement was in danger of being derailed due to the strength of opposition to women as they enter the workforce and start to really challenge men for power and status. Participating in raunch is apologising for how far we have come, Levy told her. It's as though the women contorting themselves to look like a stripper were saying to their male friends: 'Don't worry, I may compete with you for a pay rise but I'm really just a porn star.'

We're not advocating the prudish, humourless, wowser response to sex and sexuality that is sometimes – mistakenly – attributed to the F word. When Paris Hilton sued the man who put their sex tape on the Internet, she wasn't concerned about defamation; she sued for half the profits, and good for her. Young women are as entitled as young men to express their sexuality anyway they like – hopefully while practising safe sex. Our concern is that – like the fashion among teenage girls to give boys head – they don't have sex or behave in a sexually provocative fashion just to please a man. Make no mistake; a woman having sex just to please a man is a pre-feminist idea.

Feminism advocates that women should have the same freedom as men in their sexual behaviour. But there is an important addendum. It also advocates women's autonomy and control over their bodies, which is not the same as complying with a male fetish. Nor does it follow for that matter that going under the knife in an attempt to maintain your allure for men is an act of feminist self-determination. Yet in the US and increasingly Australia cosmetic surgery is now so common it's in danger of becoming de rigeur.

Observes psychoanalyist Dr Janice S. Lieberman, a specialist in narcissistic body-awareness disorders:

> Instead of working at a job, these women work on their bodies almost as a moral imperative. It's a backlash against feminism, a symptom of accelerated upward mobility, a consequence of inadequate nurturing, and a way of having control in otherwise scary times. ('The Shape of Thighs to Come', Amy Fine Collins, *Vanity Fair*, September 2007)

This adhesion to the traditional notion that equates female attractiveness with their sexual attractiveness to men – the woman as object not subject – has intensified as the march towards freedom and equality quickens. Far from being a symptom of the F word however we see the preoccupation with plastic surgery, boobs and pole dancing as a reaction against the progress feminism represents. In the same way, the feminist promise of choice has been co-opted to a very different political agenda.

Choices, choices

If women find themselves facing a dilemma because of their gender these days, society now routinely encourages them to assume it is just a personal problem, and most likely, their own fault. Women colleagues and peers often tell us how it was their 'choice' to limit their career, work part-time after having kids, or to arrange a certain type of childcare and turn themselves inside out to make sure they keep the family on the rails. But just how much choice do women really have in their lives? If they are biologically and socially encouraged to have children does that mean they then 'choose' to do all the caring for them and take the 'mummy track' at work? Or to stay at home providing the invisible labour to prop up the men in their lives? What choice do primary income-earning women have when it comes to a job and caring?

> We shouldn't confuse a bunch of decisions we make with real 'choice' that we don't have as women and mothers. It's only really a 'choice' if you have more control over the consequences. And with the current workplace and its expectations, and with an economic system where you have to fall pretty hard and far to find the safety net, mothers and fathers don't yet have control over the consequences of taking time to parent.
> (Peskowitz 2005, p. 107)

The word choice almost invariably pops up when Catherine interviews CEOs and business executives. Women don't want the top jobs, they tell her, as though these senior roles are being offered to them on a regular basis. Women make those choices and that's the way it is, the head of a large bank stated emphatically when questioned about this. It's a convenient reading of the appalling gender division at the top of most Australian organisations, and it's been helped along by the 'opting out' phenomenon which promotes the idea most women can simply leave the workplace willy nilly.

US journalist Lisa Belkin's article about well-educated women 'opting out' of high-powered jobs ('The Opt Out Revolution', *New York Times*, 26 October 2003) was greeted almost rapturously by those who never thought women should be there in the first place. The fact that the group interviewed was an elitist minority and that many didn't really 'opt out' entirely was beside the point. The article sparked controversy and the chance for the diehards to say 'I told you so'. There was plenty of choice rhetoric being bandied about by this group of women, but we never thought it added up. Why does someone with plenty of drive and ability, who has studied long and hard to get a good job, suddenly transform into a beaming Martha Stewart fan? It seemed to us the cold hard reality of modern workplaces was more the issue here.

Lo and behold, that's exactly what US academic Pamela Stone found in her research on exactly the same socio-economic group. Stone calls the 'it was my choice' rhetoric 'the illusion of choice'. Interviewing scores of women for her book *Opting Out?* she came to the conclusion that these women had very little choice at all:

> Looked at in a variety of ways, there is ample evidence
> to suggest that women did not, in fact, have many
> options about combining work and family and that they
> did not exercise a great deal of choice in deciding to
> leave their careers. (Stone 2007, p.124)

In fact, Stone says there is a choice gap between the decisions women could have made about their jobs and careers without the responsibilities of care giving, especially those around mothering, and the decisions they actually make 'to accommodate these responsibilities in light of the realities of their professions and those of their husband' (Stone 2007, p. 112).

When stripped back to show how difficult the options were even for these privileged women – many of whom had worked 60-hour weeks in their jobs before heading home – the choices don't look all that peachy.

Choice, in fact, has always been aligned with the F word but it was originally used to denote viable alternatives for women who until last century lived narrowly prescribed lives. This latest talk of choice masks a sad failure to change the fundamental order of labour all these decades on. But we think it also contributes to another trend. When the inertia at home and in jobs makes women feel like they are the problem it means they are less likely to complain. Add to this the emotion and guilt most women feel around their caring role and there's no need to tell women to shut up and get on with it – they just do. The organisations that employ us and the social expectations that stymie us are let off the hook.

Years after it was first coined the famous adage 'the personal is political' is being reversed. These days, sadly, the political is seen as personal. And it has helped to gag women effectively just when they need to be more vocal than ever.

Keeping mum

It's not just the F word that's taboo now. As a journalist writing about gender and work, Catherine has noticed a distinct retreat from public comment in the last two or three years on a whole range of gender equity issues by senior women in organisations of all kinds. The former head of a Victorian government department and ANZ executive Elizabeth Proust has spent most of her career as the lone woman in top ranks of organisations. Now a board director and executive coach, she still sees this self-censorship among women in the workplace all the time.

> Is there a level of fear about talking out? Yes, especially for a young generation. A number of people have said to me, 'I think we have got choices and if we don't like it (jobs in organisations) why would we stick around? We can go and set up a business'. But that takes you out of the potential to earn a lot of money and leaves women with low superannuation. (Interview with Elizabeth Proust)

The fear of speaking up operates at all levels in the world of paid work, and in social settings too. In organisations women quickly learn that stepping out of line or rocking the boat has unfortunate consequences. They are sidelined, miss out on promotion or find they are just ignored. Outspoken women are quickly labelled 'pushy' and attract a reputation for being difficult, as Jane knows only too well.

She has been told on many occasions by senior advertising figures that they have been warned not to use her services because she is 'a ball breaking feminist bitch'. On each of these occasions, the man in question has said that when he did employ her, this was not his experience. One bloke even said sweetly, 'But, you're not, you're just a regular Aussie girl.' Nevertheless, this labelling has definitely had an affect on her income and career. Jane couldn't shut up about feminism if you paid her, and there has been a penalty, but there have also been unexpected benefits. For women not as financially secure, silence is often the only option.

Stereotypes rule

The backlash that has produced the F word has also been helped enormously, we think, by the cultural reiteration of the myth that all women are innately very different to men in how they think and behave. An avalanche of pop psychology books and experts are surfing this lucrative trend. Stereotypes about gender are exaggerated to the point of absurdity these days. The reiteration of the 'men are from Mars, women are from Venus' mantra is unhelpful and distracting. Sure, we can see there are some behaviours that are possibly biologically driven – some to do with protecting or nurturing children for example – but the differences are minor compared to the similarities (more about this in the next chapter).

We've worked with collaborative and supportive men and dictatorial and uncommunicative women. Our husbands love to gossip with their friends and Catherine is quite handy with a power drill. A friend of ours who worked in the US for many years was often forced to correct her American business contacts if they assumed she was a laidback, easygoing Australian. This was definitely not true of her, but as with many stereotypes, quite difficult to counter. In the same way, women battle remarkably tenacious ideas about their abilities and aptitude in a range of environments, and often end up believing these messages. Women absorb these beliefs without even realising it, and feel a need to placate the men around them by taking a traditional female role even in a non-traditional setting. A very successful businesswoman tells the story of the only other female executive she works with who always pours the tea and coffee for her male colleagues and takes it on herself to make sure that any man who arrives late to the meeting is fed and watered.

Even when evidence to the contrary is staring them in the face, many women we know continue to claim they are not numerate or poor at negotiating yet they don't consider for a moment that they may have just as much innate ability but have never been encouraged, or have been routinely told they shouldn't even try because they wouldn't get it. While researching for this book, we came across a study ('Gender bias hurts employers', SHL, November 2007) of 38,000 questionnaires administered to professionals around Australia which found there were few differences between how men and women perform on the job. Duh.

Psychologist Dr Ray Glennon, Director at psychometric assessment firm SHL, studied responses to a survey completed in Australia between 2001 and 2005. He found the way people prefer to behave in the workplace is not influenced by gender.

'For example, in relation to control and leadership, some men stated they strongly dislike taking charge and prefer other team members to lead, just as some women stated they strongly like to direct and manage people,' he told us. The results also challenged other stereotypes, such as 'women dislike working with numbers' and showed there was no such thing as an 'average' male or 'average' female. There are more similarities than differences between the genders and it's not useful or reliable to apply gender stereotyping because the differences are meaningless when we look at performing on the job, Glennon said.

> Yes, stereotypes do exist and we can't pretend they
> don't. The human brain comes with the capacity to
> develop rules of thumb and it's useful to a point. But it
> becomes counter productive and they bias our decision-
> making. ('When it comes to leadership, there is no
> gender', Catherine Fox, *AFR*, 13 November 2007)

Telling women they are naturally nurturers with soft skills is not just counterproductive for women – it is insulting to men. Stereotypes operate in a space defined by resilient social norms or rules, which also punish the non-compliant. What the backlash helps to conceal is a core failure to recognise the value of women's labour. Instead of dismantling the stereotypes that hamper women the denigration of feminism often depends on reinforcing these rules.

A good example of this is occurring in the US as we write. Hillary Clinton is being battered on a daily basis by these prejudices.

Here is a woman courageous enough to seek the most powerful office in the world and boy, does she need that courage. There is a special set of words used exclusively to describe women who ask for more, be it attention, money, power or high office. These words include 'strident', 'shrill', 'peevish', 'nagging', 'demanding' and 'hysterical'. Many of these have been used regularly to describe Hillary Clinton, particularly as her campaign faltered. The only positive adjective we've been able to find is 'plucky' which is at best condescending. She alone among the candidates has to face a set of standards and a level of scrutiny unprecedented in normal all-male presidential races. Even her closest opponent, African-American Senator Barack Obama ('cool' and 'authoritative' according to the same article that called Clinton 'peevish'), has not faced the same pressure. It seems to us that the leadership battle in America shows gender stereotypes are even more punitive than those of race. Judgments about gender are immobilising. Hillary Clinton can't win, even if she becomes the Democrats' presidential nominee. If she is seen as a stereotypical woman she will be judged weak and not up to the job; if not, she will be judged as a hard-faced bitch. No wonder women are reluctant to put their hand up for leadership positions.

Hillary Clinton's dilemma reflects the dilemma of feminism itself. Just like the women it seeks to free, feminism has become a victim of polarisation. Either it is weak and past its use-by date, or it has produced selfish, family-wrecking bitches. Far from being seen as a blessing, feminism has become a curse. The most damaging of these dichotomies is the idea that one can only be pro-female (feminist) by being anti-male. This is nonsense, but tenacious.

Thanks to these extremes the positive impact of feminism on women's lives has been undervalued and undermined as the word progressively turned into a term of abuse.

All those years ago, when we got excited about our educational prospects and jobs, we attributed our widening horizons to feminism. Along with our friends, we saw we had better lives and were proud to be called feminist, particularly after we became mothers. 'We no longer need to worry about whether one can be a feminist and a mother at the same time; we know that's a false opposition.' (Peskowitz 2005, p. 148) The false dichotomy attributed to feminism is in fact just a rewording of the ancient dichotomy that women have always struggled with. Women, unlike men, are restricted by rigid expectations and judgments; madonna/whore, good mother/bad mother, housewife/career woman, Miss/Mrs, submissive/aggressive. The feminism we are grateful for has helped us shrug off these narrow definitions, but there is still more to be done.

A new feminism is what the next chapter is all about.

12

Reclaiming the F word

Before we look at a new feminism, it is worthwhile taking a moment to think about the remarkable success the women's movement has achieved since 18th-century British feminist Mary Wollstonecraft – no doubt in white hot fury – dipped her pen into an inkwell in 1792 and began to put words to the injustice she experienced. Without her cri de coeur *Vindication of the Rights of Women* and all the remarkable work of women who came after her, our lives would be very different.

In the last 300 years, women like us have gained the right to their own money and to their own children. They have gained the right to be educated, to vote, to choose their own employment and, in theory at least, to go as far in the world as their talents and determination will take them. They have gained the right to say yes and no to sex, and yes and no to marriage. They can control their own bodies and their fertility; they can live alone or with one another. They can stand for high office, sit in parliament, in judgment over other men and women and preach the gospel.

They can preside over the fate of great nations and go into battle side by side with male colleagues. They fly planes, pilot rockets, drive cars, perform brain surgery and build bridges. Just about anything a man does, there is a woman somewhere doing it too. All the old rationalisations that limited women – they are not physically/intellectually as strong, it will affect their ability to reproduce, there are not enough female toilets, they are not 'tough' enough – have, if not entirely disappeared, at least dwindled in significance.

And all along women have been discussing that journey: in conversation, in letters, in fiction and non-fiction, in newspapers and films, in diaries and the stories they tell, thus creating a mosaic of female experience and testimony. We've tried to analyse the touch points where feminism has had an impact on our lives: as we were growing up; in our families and at school; through role models and in watching the progress – and inertia – of women's rights; in making sense of gender roles at home and work; in our marriages and with our children; in our autonomy over our bodies and the way we thought about our place in the world; and by looking at the tragedy for women who have access to none of feminism's great bequests.

Ridiculed and discounted at the time, Wollstonecraft's ability to see glaring injustice when society was utterly blind to it marked the beginning of and remains the major purpose of feminism. It is fundamentally about seeing the world from a female perspective. Wollstonecraft's great contribution was that she articulated the constraints under which women were forced to live their lives. The struggle to remove those constraints has never been straightforward and progress has ebbed and flowed.

Could we go backwards?

Looking back over three centuries of feminism, a pattern emerges. It takes a great deal of courage and energy for women to move forwards against entrenched and often unconscious resistance. Once the barriers have been pushed back, it takes just as much energy to keep them at bay. Women have lost (and in some parts of the world, are still losing) their lives in this fight. Understandably, women get tired, because we're holding back these barriers while also doing all the things women have always done. And when our energy is depleted, the old ways, the old prejudices and some of the old restrictions reappear. Worse, events outside our control also affect the fight for women's rights; economic downturns, wars and political upheaval all stymie our progress. Interestingly, we never lose everything we have gained, but the freedoms we hang on to tend to be the ones that suit the power structure of the time. The most recent example is the flood of educated women into the paid workforce over the last three decades just as market economies needed them.

This push-pull was also evident during WWII when many women supported the war effort by working in non-traditional occupations, which, of course, were much better paid than traditional female occupations. Postwar came the backlash and women were once again banished to the suburbs. Even the fashions changed and became more constricting, with stilettos, wasp waists and anatomically impossible pointy breasts the order of the day. Women flooded back into their homes and maternity, not always without complaint, but because it was still believed to be their place. Such a setback didn't last much longer than a decade or two, however, before women were burning those same bras and girdles and demanding the right to their own jobs, lives and orgasms. Despite this two steps forward, one step back rhythm, we would argue that on the whole, the concepts that underpin feminism have become more mainstream in our society. This is particularly evident when you look at the lives of women in some cultures.

As we pointed out in Chapter 10, women outside developed nations have indeed been going backwards – and fast. Recently Professor Pervez Hoodbhoy from Quaid-e-Azam University in Islamabad spoke to Phillip Adams ('Late Night Live', Radio National, 29 August 2007) about the changes he had witnessed teaching students. When he first began his career at the university, 35 years ago, very few of his female students – almost all of whom were Muslim – wore any kind of veil. Now virtually all of them wear the most extreme kind: the black chador, which covers every part of a woman's body except her hands and eyes. His concern about this change is that it has affected the way his female students participate in learning. Three decades ago, he said, his unveiled female students were active participants in class discussions; now they have become silent, black-clad note-takers.

Yes, we can and often do slip backwards or our expectations are not met. Social change is like that; it's unpredictable, it's dynamic and sometimes it blindsides you. As we've argued, it is essential that the forward momentum of this great human rights tradition continues. And as educated, privileged Western women are the primary beneficiaries of this movement, it is our responsibility to make sure it thrives and that its benefits are more evenly distributed.

When we are asked by younger women in Australia about

the failure of feminism to advance as quickly or logically as they expect, we explain that on the contrary the relative speed of change in recent decades is an aberration and not the other way around. As a result there is an enormous gap between what contemporary women expect and what they actually get. A young female lawyer expecting her first child told us she had resigned from her job when it was made abundantly clear she would get little support from her employer and would probably be demoted. 'We should be marching in the streets,' she said, still in shock at the way her life was turning out.

Those not as privileged are much worse off, rendered silent by their vulnerability. The many women in low-paid and casual jobs who were either sacked or lost pay and conditions under the Howard Government's controversial WorkChoices legislation were in no position to fight back. A study on the impact of Workchoices from the University of Sydney released in July 2007 not only found women were suffering particularly under the new laws but had internalised many of the changes and felt powerless and fearful as a result ('The voiceless victims', Marian Baird and Rae Cooper, *Sydney Morning Herald*, 31 July 2007). Many women are familiar with this anxiety and marginalisation no matter where they sit in the social hierarchy, but if it is our responsibility to keep feminism alive, how do we overcome our fears?

The getting of wisdom

1. Speak up.

Our experience over many years tells us that conversations about these topics are taking place throughout our communities: in cafes, workplaces, supermarkets and mothers' groups; and that's great, but it's not enough. We have been lucky to be asked to share our experiences publicly and it's clear from the response we get that our explorations provide context for the frustrations many women encounter. Even more importantly, we believe that by talking about our own struggles, we help women realise they are not alone; nor are their responses either imaginary or exaggerated. Over and over again, it seems to us, women have to fight to have their feelings and experiences taken seriously and not dismissed as trivial, foolish or over-dramatic.

Despite the scorn and ridicule, speaking only to one another or staying quiet is no longer an option. If women don't speak up, we don't just lose the chance for change; we run the risk of losing what we already have. There may be a short-term advantage, or even safety, in keeping quiet, but there is a heavy long-term price to be paid. We have to stop apologising for ourselves, and for our rights, or waiting for someone to notice and reward our hard work, and start standing up and demanding them. And support one another when we do so.

2. Give yourself a break.

Almost every woman we spoke to while researching this book said they felt life was better for women now than it had been when they were growing up and much better than it was for their mothers' generation. Some had mothers who had struggled on their own to care for them while working full-time, others had mums who were full-time housewives, and some mums had returned to work or study after their children grew up. Many women we interviewed spoke of their mothers' hopes for them, but also of the older women's envy of their new opportunities to study and work and enjoy financial independence.

One woman we interviewed, who is approaching 50 and has two children, said she was sure life was better for her and would be even better for her daughters, but she had reservations. Her own mother she told us was glad that the world had changed for women but often remarked on how busy her daughter's life had become, with so many different activities to fit in around paid and unpaid work.

This pressure on time has become an underlying theme in much of the modern literature and discourse on feminism. It's a discussion about the double shift and the pressure from rapacious workplaces, but it's also about time for yourself. The truth is, when we switched to part-time work our rationale was not entirely based on spending extra hours with children, although that played some part in our decisions. We're not selfless saints and we wanted to avoid exhaustion and circumvent the martyrdom trap. But most of all, we wanted to live as well as to work. This is crucial for both men and women and has come to us from feminism.

As social researcher Hugh Mackay puts it:

> Women have been trying to develop a new way of thinking about work. But as the revolution matures, it may turn out to have been more about sanity – balance, values, clarifying the meaning and purpose of our lives – than about gender. (Mackay 2007, p.39)

3. Value what you do.

The dynamics of family life and the demands made on women are only just starting to be seriously explored. These are not topics that have been deemed particularly deserving of scrutiny until now. The work we have quoted throughout this book, by US authors Arlie Hochschild and Joan Williams, Australians such as Barbara Pocock, Michael Bittman, Hugh Mackay and Anne Summers and organisations such as the Human Rights and Equal Opportunity Commission, Equal Opportunity for Women in the Workplace Agency and the Diversity Council do more than provide invaluable analysis, data and research on time and effort and responsibility. They form an overlapping picture of what is occurring in the private lives of Australians, and the implications for us all. And they validate the need for more discussion and research to show us the interconnections of the social roles women inhabit and the complexity of their agendas. We'd even go so far as to suggest that in our technologically-enabled and globalised world, women may turn out to have the multitasking skills – because of the variety of roles they routinely juggle – that will be crucial to our future.

When we are asked our thoughts on the challenges women face we often mention the need to stop trying to run our lives as though they are neatly compartmentalised. A woman's additional emotional concerns about the family or an elderly parent don't suddenly switch off when she leaves the home or goes to a job. The first step towards placing a value on caring and emotional labour is actually to recognise that they are happening and legitimise them as work, rather than fob them off as love.

4. Don't blame yourself.

Learning to shrug off the weight of the outdated expectations and absurd double standards that apply to women is not easy. A woman in an executive role told us that when faced with traditional gender barriers she reminds herself: 'It shouldn't matter.' Indeed it shouldn't, but it often does.

Feminism has given us the tools to understand the complex interplay of our lives, society and prejudice that causes so many women to feel responsible for factors they have no control over. Once, female suffering and misery was just a given – their lot, so to speak, ordained by God. Now, women still suffer, but we are beginning to understand we are not helpless. Eradicating the need for that stoicism and self-blame is the essence of what the empowerment of women is all about.

We understand however why women are so vulnerable to such self-defeating behaviour – we are not immune to it ourselves. But when one of us threatens to slip into self-pity or worse, self-loathing, the other is quick to point it out. This is one of the powerful ways women sustain one another, and therefore is probably the nemesis of the pharmaceutical industry. Women supporting women is as effective as prozac, and has no side effects.

5. There's no silver bullet.

There's been a torrent of advice for women over the last few years on how to get ahead and wise up to the way the world works. Worryingly, much of this self-help information tells women to accept reality, learn the male rules and never complain. Or it advocates a facial and some time out. Well meaning they may be, but these packaged formulas are bandaid solutions at best and at worst, they support the status quo but never challenge the social order that perpetuates unfairness.

> If female fear and self-doubt were ever eradicated, the publishing industry would collapse. Another day, another book or magazine article about how women can have better orgasms, more money, smarter kids; mix job and family, spirituality and ambition; be a feminist and a stripper. But no matter the issue, the premise is pretty much the same: We're doing something wrong. ('The Feminine Mistake', Joan Walsh, <salon.com>, 3 April 2007)

This theme of blaming half the human race for their own misfortunes seems particularly persistent. Fortunately feminism is helping many women to see that no matter how many hoops they jump through, how good they look, how neat the house is, or how hard they work, they will only get so far.

Women are beginning to understand the need for structural as well as social and individual change. As we've said, we feel the incursions women have made into the public sphere and those that men have made into the domestic arena are significant signs of progress. And this broadening of valid options for both genders is an important illustration of feminism's power to enrich us all. Nevertheless, we remain cautious about unrealistic expectations. We've lived long enough to realise that there is no panacea.

7. Have a laugh.

> I think print journalism is a great career for women.
> There are some dinosaurs around but they are generally
> slow-moving and easy to sidestep. What barriers have I
> encountered? Well, the electronic security tag is the bane
> of my existence. I cannot keep one for more than about
> three seconds. This is a serious barrier which I have
> encountered in a number of jobs. The sooner I can be
> microchipped the better. (Annabel Crabb, email interview)

Thank God for women like Annabel Crabb. They remind us that
the very fact that half the human race has to struggle for the rights
the other half enjoy is absurd. A sense of humour relies heavily
on a sense of proportion, the ability to see yourself and what you
believe in relation to the rest of the world. Humour is by its very
nature subversive. It questions and doubts and points out the
gaps between the rhetoric of the powerful and their actions. Most
importantly, if you can laugh at yourself it's much harder to feel
like a victim or a martyr. No wonder women are so funny.

Where to from here?

We have never been in doubt that heterosexual men are the victims
as much as they are the beneficiaries of sexism. We pity the lack of
contact so many men have with their children, we worry about the
relative shortness of men's lives, we fear the stoicism that makes
them unable to care for themselves properly. We get angry about
but also empathise with their fear of displaying any weakness or

vulnerability. And we are saddened by the plight of small boys who – from the day they are born – are culturally restricted in what colours they may wear and what toys they may play with. Society has learnt to admire the feisty tomboy, but still fears and despises the sissy.

Within feminism, we believe, is the key to broadening the choices and opportunities of heterosexual men. When feminism took off in the 1960s and '70s, there was a concurrent trend for men to grow their hair, and it enraged the older generation. In a way, we understand why our fathers hated it. Long hair was about freedom – freedom to feel. It symbolised that men were becoming more accepting of their feminine side – of their emotions, their vulnerability, their humanity.

In a similar way, the men's health movement, exemplified by campaigns like 'mo-vember' (where men are encouraged to grow a moustache in November) which draw attention to male depression and suicide, and the new attention around prostate cancer, are examples of activism inspired by feminism. The fuss about the boys who fail at school is also indicative of a fresh understanding by men that they need to draw attention to the parts of society that don't work for them and actively agitate for change. Just as women have realised no one is going to rescue them, so it is for men. Perhaps the most important symbolic lesson gained from the success of feminism is that nothing is immutable – injustices, no matter how long-standing or how ingrained, can be reduced, and women have proved it.

If the liberation of women can only be achieved alongside the liberation of men, then there are more than enough reasons for our husbands, lovers, fathers, brothers and sons to involve themselves in the fight by our side. Women want more rights, certainly, but we are also happy to shoulder our fair share of responsibilities. We want to succeed and are prepared to fail as long as the measures applied to us are no higher or lower than those applied to anyone else. We don't want the accident of our gender to dictate our fate. Nothing about these aspirations is ridiculous or unreasonable, but we know we will only achieve them incrementally, and that old conditioning and prejudices die hard. We can cope with that, we can even forgive it. But when these baseless assumptions are pointed out, we don't want to be blamed for them or ridiculed or made to feel as if we are neurotic, needy and mad.

There is an old question, rarely voiced these days, but nevertheless running as an undercurrent beneath the squabbles and misunderstandings that occur in households, workplaces and universities on a daily basis. 'What do women want?' has been asked in a bewildered, almost exasperated, tone since women first began to say they wanted more. Yet the answer seems to us to be simple and entirely self-evident. Women want what all sentient human beings want. They want to develop their own talents and put them to good use, to earn and control their own money so they can be truly independent and make free choices. They want to gain status and respect as they prove to be worthy of it. To love and to be loved as free and equal adults, to be allowed their human flaws and foibles and not to be unfairly judged for them, and to be forgiven when they fail, behave badly or have trouble coping. To be the subject and not the object. They want, in short, what men want.

When feminists spoke of equality at home, in the community

and on the job it was pounced on by those who said, gleefully, that women would never be the equal to men because they bear children and are not physically as strong. But equal does not mean the same, it means of comparable value. Equality of opportunity is not a clarion call to erase gender differences and make men and women interchangeable. The goal of the feminism we swear by is for women to inhabit the full spectrum of human behaviour and endeavour. The new feminism says that men should be able to do so too.

A new feminism

Until now, feminism needed to be a movement for, by and about women because women were so peculiarly and unfairly constrained and governed by their sex. However, by seeking to broaden the options women had, by seeking to help them to develop their potential and their freedom, the movement became a model for the liberation of many others as well.

Feminists were active in fighting for the end of slavery; they were (and are) active in the fight against racism; and feel a particular affinity with the fight by homosexuals and lesbians to gain their full rights as human beings. Having been defined by something they could not change for so long (their sex) many women have learnt to understand intuitively the desire of others defined by equally unchangeable characteristics – race, class and sexual orientation – for freedom.

Human society has spent the last 2000 years emphasising and exaggerating the differences between men and women. It has created religious traditions, laws, cultures, pogroms, torture chambers and superstitions to delineate and control the differences. Policing them has caused much grief, pain and suffering. It has also robbed the world of half its available talent, something we can afford to waste no longer.

In our own lives, we have used feminism to help us make sense of many barriers because it shed so much light on our concerns and helped us see beyond the *what* to the *why*. We were the fortunate beneficiaries of all the advantages earlier feminists fought for. And we say thank you on a daily basis. But the time has come for feminism to evolve yet again, as it has done so effectively in the past. We're not advocating a return to the feminism of the 1960s and '70s, nor are we advocating walking away from what it has achieved. The principles of feminism – the right of women to full human rights – have not changed, but the way ahead requires a new, inclusive strategy.

Feminism has been getting a lot of bad press lately, allowing some of its core concerns to slip silently off the agenda. The fact that it has become the F word, and that so many of its direct beneficiaries actively reject it, both as a label and as a philosophy, is a signal that it needs rejuvenation. Feminism is all too often seen as divisive and as a wedge between the genders. And this adversarial image has done enormous damage, pitting women against other women through constructs such as the 'mummy wars', and against men. That's not a 21st century way of thinking.

However, we see signs that a new feminism is slowly evolving: a feminism that is beginning to concentrate on getting us all to understand what we have in common. That is not only interested in the wrongs done to women, but in the shared humanity of us all. Feminism is not a dirty word. It has a proud and remarkable past. It can list achievements of a revolutionary and universally beneficial nature. Without it, quite frankly, where would any of us be? We must not give up the principles of feminism, or the word itself. It is up to the educated, privileged and relatively secure women of the world to reclaim the word and proudly identify with it. 'I am a feminist' is then something we would hear a lot more often, from both women and men.

At the very beginning of this book we listed the many often contradictory criticisms that women like us seem to attract. No matter which way we turn it can seem there is someone just waiting to wag their finger and tut tut at us in disapproval. Yet when we think about all the women we know – young and old, married and single, mothers and non-mothers, in the paid workforce or not – we see far more to admire than to criticise. We belong to a generation of women who are living their lives in an entirely new way. Change is always scary and no doubt we have all made and will continue to make plenty of mistakes, but the old ways simply weren't working for women any more.

Mothers in particular are charting new territory, juggling parenting and housekeeping with paid work. We are creating a new way to be married, a new look workplace and a new and, we believe, much healthier way for men and women to relate to one another romantically, professionally and as fellow human beings. We will all get lots of things wrong, but what women are doing is exciting, courageous and fundamentally important for all of us, but particularly for the women and men who will come after us.

Like most mothers, when we get together the constant topic of conversation at our coffee mornings is our children, all of whom are girls. We whinge about them, boast about them and of course worry about them. As they grow up and begin to express their own opinions, they have begun to challenge us. They see few barriers in their future. The idea that they are in anyway lesser than any other person is alien to them. We wonder, should we warn them or let them find out for themselves? It will be harder to convince them to shut up, take less pay and live half a life. As they fall in and out of love we are heartened by the change in the way young men and women relate to one another, and we notice that this change of tone is often set by the girls. They will have their own sets of problems no doubt and their own relationship with feminism, but, we hope, as feminists we have given them the skills and confidence they need to deal with whatever life throws at them.

Bibliography

Baumgardner, Jennifer, Smyth, C, Rawsthorne M and Siminski P *Women's Lifework: Labour market transition experiences of women*, Sydney, Social Policy Research Centre, UNSW (Final report August 2005)

Bergman, Barbara (1988) *The Economic Emergence of Women*, New York: Basic Books

Bonnor, Chris & Caro, Jane (2007) *The Stupid Country: How Australia is dismantling public education*, Sydney: UNSW Press

Bravo, Ellen (2007) *Taking on the Big Boys*, New York: First Feminist Press

Chick, Suzanne (1994) *Searching for Charmian,* Australia: Macmillan

Commonwealth of Australia, House of Representatives Standing Committee on Family and Human Services, 'Balancing Work and Family: Report on the inquiry into balancing work and family', Canberra (December 2006)

Couprie, Helene, 'Time Allocation Within the Family: Welfare implications of life in a couple', London, *Economic Journal* (January 2007)

De Beauvoir, Simone (1989) translated by H.M. Pashley, *The Second Sex,* New York: Vintage Books

Ehrenreich, Barbara (2000) 'Maid to Order: The politics of other women's work', *Harper's Magazine* (April 1, 2000)

Ephron, Nora (2006) *I Feel Bad About my Neck*, London: Black Swan

Equal Opportunity for Women in the Workplace Agency (2006) *Australian Census of Women in Leadership*, Sydney, EOWA

Farrelly, Elizabeth (2007) *Blubberland,* Sydney: UNSW Press

Friedan, Betty (2002) *The Feminine Mystique*, New York: W.W. Norton &

Company

Garner, Helen (1995) *The First Stone*, Sydney: Pan Macmillan

Haussegger, Virginia (2005) *Wonder Women: The myth of 'having it all'*, Sydney: Allen & Unwin

Hochschild, Arlie (2003) *The Commercialization of Intimate Life: Notes from home and work*, Berkeley: University of California Press

Levitt, Steven D. and Dubner, Stephen J. (2005) *Freakonomics*, New York: William Morrow

Levy, Ariel (2005) *Female Chauvinist Pigs: Women and the rise of raunch culture*, New York: Schwartz

Mackay, Hugh (2007) *Advance Australia ... Where?* Sydney: Hachette Australia

Manne, Anne (2005) *Motherhood: How should we care for our children?* Sydney: Allen & Unwin

Ogden, Christopher (1994) *Life of the Party: The biography of Pamela Digby Churchill Hayward Harriman*, New York: Little, Brown & Company

Peskowitz, Miriam (2005) *The Truth behind the Mommy Wars*, New York: Seal Press

Pocock, Barbara (2003) *The Work/Life Collision: What work is doing to Australians and what to do about it*, Sydney: Federation Press

Rose, Phyllis (1984) *Parallel Lives*, London: Chatto & Windus, The Hogarth Press

Siegel, Deborah (2007) *Sisterhood, Interrupted: From radical women to grrls gone wild*, New York: Palgrave Macmillan

Stone, Pamela (2007) *Opting Out?* Berkeley: University of California Press

Stopes, Marie Carmicheal (1918) *Married Love*, New York: The Critic and Guide Company

Summers, Anne (2003) *The End of Equality*, Sydney: Random House

Summers, Anne (2002) *Damned Whores and Gods Police*, Sydney: Penguin

Traister, Rebecca *Chicks Behind Flicks*, <salon.com> (11 October 2007)

Wheatley, Nadia (2001) *The Life and Myth of Charmian Clift*, Australia: Harper Collins

Williams, Joan (2000) *Unbending Gender*, New York: Oxford University Press

Withius, Jolande *Shoot the Women First, Part 3*, <newmatilda.com> (5 November 2007)

Wollstonecraft, Mary (1792) *A Vindication of the Rights of Woman*, Boston: Thomas and Andrews

Woolf, Virginia (1929) *A Room of One's Own*, London: Hogarth Press

Index